AN ESSAY

ON THE

DOCTRINE OF CONTRACTS;

BEING

AN INQUIRY

HOW CONTRACTS ARE AFFECTED

IN LAW AND MORALS,

BY

CONCEALMENT, ERROR, OR INADEQUATE PRICE.

BY GULIAN C VERPLANCK.

"Quod SEMPER Æquum et Bonum, Jus dicitur."
Digest. L. 11. de Just. et Jure.

THE LAWBOOK EXCHANGE, LTD.
Clark, New Jersey
2006

ISBN-13: 978-1-58477-637-6
ISBN-10: 1-58477-637-4

The quality of this reprint is equivalent to the quality of the original work.
Printed in the United States of America on acid-free paper

THE LAWBOOK EXCHANGE, LTD.
33 Terminal Avenue
Clark, New Jersey 07066-1321

Please see our website for a selection of our other publications and fine facsimile reprints of classic works of legal history:
www.lawbookexchange.com

Library of Congress Cataloging-in-Publication Data

Verplanck, Gulian C. (Gulian Crommelin), 1786-1870.
An essay on the doctrine of contracts : being an inquiry how contracts are affected in law and morals by concealment, error, or inadequate price / Gulian C. Verplanck.
p. cm.
Originally published: New York : Published By G. & C. Carvill, 1825.
Includes bibliographical references.
ISBN 1-58477-637-4 (alk. paper)
1. Illegal contracts--United States. 2. Immoral contracts--United States. 3. Fraud--United States. 4. Mistake (Law)--United States.
I. Title.

KF817.V45 2005
346.7302--dc22 2005015353

AN ESSAY

ON THE

DOCTRINE OF CONTRACTS;

BEING

AN INQUIRY

HOW CONTRACTS ARE AFFECTED

IN LAW AND MORALS,

BY

CONCEALMENT, ERROR, OR INADEQUATE PRICE.

BY GULIAN C VERPLANCK.

" Quod SEMPER Æquum et Bonum, Jus dicitur."
Digest. L. 11. *de Just. et Jure.*

NEW-YORK:
PUBLISHED BY G. & C. CARVILL.

G. F. Hopkins, Printer.

PREFACE.

The necessity of absence from home for several months, and the approach of public duties which may leave little leisure for other studies, induced the author to begin to print the following Essay before he had completed it; and to hurry it through the press with as little delay as might be.

Hence have arisen some,—perhaps many,—inaccuracies of style and of reference, though none, it is hoped, at all essential to the reasoning or the sense. From the same cause, the argument is often less clearly stated and fully developed, than might have been done, had greater leisure permitted a more deliberate revision.

For these imperfections the author must request the reader's indulgence. With respect to the truth of his main doctrine, he has no right to claim indulgence, nor does he ask it. His opinions were formed with much deliberation, without any interest or prejudice to bias or mislead him, and with all the aids which could be derived from the command of good libraries, some opportunity of practical observation, and much acquaintance with judicious and experienced men of business.

Without being fully satisfied with the manner in which he has treated the subject, he is deeply impressed with a sense of the truth and value of his general doctrine; and should he succeed in awakening the public mind to the conviction of the necessity of making our law of Sales and Contracts perfectly rational and consistent, he feels assured that he will have done good service to his country.

At any rate,—he trusts that the confidence which the inhabitants of this great and commercial city have repeatedly reposed in him, by electing him as their Representative in the State and National Legislatures, will authorize and enable him to call their attention to the serious consideration of some points in the Morals of Trade, regarding which false legal maxims and erroneous usages have combined to mislead many who would not wilfully do wrong.

With these hopes and feelings, the Author respectfully dedicates this Essay

TO

HIS NATIVE CITY,

TO WHICH HE IS BOUND BY EVERY TIE

OF

AFFECTION AND GRATITUDE.

NEW-YORK, *November* 25, 1825.

CONTENTS.

ERRATUM.

At page 70 strike out the sentence beginning with "It seems" to the end of the paragraph, and insert as follows, viz.

"This (says Pothier,) seems to me wrong, as the vendor is himself quite free to sell or not to sell, he ought to leave the buyer perfectly free to buy or not to buy, even at a fair price, if that price does not suit the buyer: it is unjust to lay a snare for this liberty which the buyer ought equally to enjoy, by concealing from him the faults in order to induce him to buy what otherwise he would not have been willing to purchase at that rate, knowing its defects."

CHAPTER I.

Statement of the question....Some of its difficulties suggested....The importance of a sound and uniform rule....Disagreement concerning it in the rules and decisions of Law.

We all remember, that just at the conclusion of the late war between Great Britain and the United States, the issue of the negotiation then pending between the American and British commissioners at Ghent, was generally considered very doubtful; and many of those in both countries whose interests were most affected by the war wholly despaired of peace. In this state of public opinion, a few days after the memorable attack upon New-Orleans, and whilst the British fleet and army were still in the neighbourhood of that city, official intelligence that a treaty of peace had been actually signed was received on board the fleet, and was there communicated to two or three American merchants who were accidentally on board. They immediately brought the news to New-Orleans.

That the event should have taken place at the very time which it did, was unexpected every where; and must have been wholly so at New-Orleans, which had, within a few weeks, been the anxious scene of the most daring and bloody operations of the whole war.

From the blockade of the American ports, and the command of the whole coast by the superior naval force of the enemy; from the difficulty, and in some cases impossibility, of internal transportation from one extremity of the union to the other, and the entire closing of the best and usual foreign markets for the staple commodities of the southern states,—the price of cotton, rice, and tobacco had fallen to the lowest ebb, and in fact would have become nearly nominal, had not hopes of a return of peace and commerce at some future, though distant period, given them a little prospective value; since all were confident, that whenever peace was restored, it would bring with it brisk trade and high prices.

The intelligence of peace was brought up to the city on the very night it was received; and soon after sunrise the next morning, before it could possibly be at all known among men of business, a merchant, who had just been put in possession of the information, called upon another in the same branch of trade, and without giving him any hint of the news, (but at the same time without asserting or suggesting any thing calculated to impose upon him, or to induce a belief that no such event had occurred or was expected,) contracted for the purchase of a large quantity of tobacco at the market price of the day before.

Immediately after, and altogether in consequence of the peace, the price of tobacco rose more than fifty per cent.

It will naturally occur to every thinking man to ask, Was this a fair transaction? Does it square with the rules of honourable dealing among merchants, or even of common honesty among men?

The lawyer and the man of business will besides be led to inquire, Whether or no this could be a valid sale? Is not the suppression of a fact, so essential to the fixing the value of that and all similar commodities,—a fact too, within the positive knowledge of the buyer, and not accessible to the seller,—equivalent to a fraud? And if so, upon that great and fundamental principle of the law of contracts, that good faith is necessary to the validity of all agreements, must not such a suppression furnish sufficient legal ground to release the seller from his contract, or to relieve him in damages if it were already executed?

Again; independently of fraud, a doubt may arise, (especially among those acquainted with the principles of the civil law, and the decisions of Chancery,) whether or no the gross inadequacy of price at the time of delivery were not alone sufficient to claim the aid of equity to rescind so unequal a bargain?

The litigation which actually grew out of this transaction involved some other points of positive and local law; but when finally carried up to the supreme court of the United States, the argument turned mainly upon the question first above stated. In delivering the opinion of the court, Chief Justice Marshal said: "The question in this case is, whe-
" ther the intelligence of extraneous circumstances
" which might influence the price of the commodi-
" ty, and which was exclusively within the know-
" ledge of the vendee, ought to have been commu-
" nicated by him to the Vendor? *The court is of*
" *opinion that he was not bound to communicate it.*
" It would be difficult to circumscribe the contrary
" doctrine within proper limits, where the means of
" intelligence are equally accessible to both parties.
" But at the same time each party must take care
" not to say or do any thing tending to impose upon
" the other."*

Such is the law, as authoritatively laid down by the highest judicial tribunal of the United States, and pronounced by a judge whose character and genius would do honour to any country or any station. But it is much to be regretted that the deci-

* Laidlaw *v* Organ. II. Wheaton, 195.

sion is stated in this brief and general manner, unaccompanied by the reasoning or authority upon which it was founded, and without any statement of the extent to which the doctrine is applicable, or any suggestion of the limitations which might be necessary to guard it from abuse.

If the Chief Justice had applied his logical and original mind to the deliberative and argumentative examination of this subject in all its bearings, this case would have afforded him an admirable opportunity to investigate and settle upon some broad and uniform principles, the important and difficult question of the nature and degree of equality in compensation, in skill or in knowledge, required between the parties to any contract of mutual benefit, (and particularly, of bargain and sale,) in order to make it valid in law, or just and right in private conscience.

However correct this judicial decision may have been in point of law, and however strongly the expediency of the law, as laid down, may seem to be recommended by considerations of public policy and the necessities of trade, yet I believe, most of those who, without much speculation or deliberate reasoning, form their moral judgments from their unstudied impressions of right and wrong, will find it somewhat revolting to their notions of sound morality. It frequently happens in the common affairs of life, that cases similar to this occur, where, without any falsehood or positive fraud, by mere silence, the superior information of one party is liberally rewarded at the heavy expense of the other.

In most of these cases, ingenuous minds, unhackneyed in the ways of men, and unaccustomed to argue away their first warm impressions, have little hesitation to pronounce such advantages to be dishonourable frauds, or at best, base and ungenerous tricks.

It does not follow as a matter of course that such opinions must be correct; yet it cannot well be, but that the feelings which prompt them, and the principles to which they are referred, should not have some sanction from truth and reason.

Indeed many cases of this nature might be imagined, where no one could hesitate in deciding as to their dishonesty. We may suppose that an ignorant woman has by accident a bank note of large amount, which she sells as a mere curiosity to a person who knows its worth, but uses no other artifice of deception than that of not telling the real value of her piece of engraved paper.

A farmer, ignorant of the manner and time of drawing lotteries, and living at a distance from the city where they are drawn, has a ticket: his crafty neighbour learns from the city newspapers, which the other never sees, that that number has drawn the high prize, and without communicating the news, buys it at a small advance on its first cost; the owner supposing it still undrawn, the buyer using no other art than silence, and not undeceiving him.

These, most men would at once pronounce to be frauds, and would look upon any system of law as disgracefully defective if it did not afford an adequate relief. In truth, no better proof of the universal agreement of the decisions of untutored moral feeling in such cases, need be required, than is furnished by the indignation which is so frequently excited by any intentional overcharge of the retail tradesman, upon those whose ignorance may put them in his power.

If a foreigner or an ignorant servant should be induced to pay to a shopkeeper for his goods three or four times the price at which they are sold to other people, no one hesitates to say that this is a cheat. Though such cases may not appear in the courts, yet whenever they occur, the fraud is punished by public opinion, and generally too, practically and efficiently in the way of business, by the injured party and others withdrawing their custom.

Opinions thus general, and apparently so natural, seldom spring from caprice or accidental prejudice. They are commonly the spontaneous result of the moral observations and experience of our whole lives. We may find ourselves incapable of analyzing them into their elements; still they are irresistible in their conviction.

Yet decided and clear as our opinions may be in this or any similar case, the moment we begin to reason upon the subject with a view of reducing it to some general rules, we shall find it to present many difficulties, and to involve apparent contradictions.

If I cannot,—it may reasonably be asked,—if I cannot honestly take advantage of my better knowledge of some fact which regulates the value of a purchase or sale, can I then more justly take advantage of my superior sagacity, of my superior skill in the particular trade, or my superior general knowledge of commerce?

Lawyers and divines* have said that all bargains are made under the idea of giving and receiving equivalents in value. Now then, they add, if the seller by being better informed about the true value of the thing sold than the purchaser, or from any other cause, should obtain more for it than it is worth; or if for want of equality of knowledge, or from accident, the buyer should get it for too little; in either case, one party has not received that equivalent which was the condition of the transfer, and consequently the contract must fail.

Here again, we must pause to ask, Can this be true, without many exceptions? Is this exact equality either in knowledge or value always possible in the nature of things? Can there then be no such thing as an advantageous bargain which is at

* See Grotius, Puffendorf, Rutherford, Barbeyrac.

the same time an honest one?—no such thing in trade as a fair and virtuous employment of sagacity and foresight? It certainly cannot be essential to the making of a fair bargain, that before I can deal with my indolent neighbour, I should communicate to him all my private plans, my long-sighted views of the future state of the market, my surmises—in short, all the results of that knowledge and address which have been the hard earned acquisitions of my own industry and activity. My knowledge of the articles in which I traffic, and of the circumstances which influence the fluctuations of their market price, forms the most valuable and perhaps the most costly part of my capital. Why then are not the profits which I may make by using them as much my own, as the interest of my money or the rents of my houses?

Moreover, does not public policy agree with common sense, in allowing the skilful and industrious the full enjoyment of that necessary superiority over their competitors, which well directed industry must always give?

Again: If he who purchases a diamond or a bank note from an ignorant owner, for a few shillings, is bound either in law or conscience to relinquish his gains; why does not the same rule hold as to every other profitable bargain?

Ought not, for instance, the purchaser of real estate, who looking forward with a more enlightened foresight than his neighbours, has bought for a trifle, (but at its current price at the time of sale,) the land which the increase of trade and population has since made worth millions—ought not he too to refund his gains?

If the policy of the law hinder it from interfering here, to compel restitution, yet may not the decision of conscience be different, and call upon him to divide his profits?

It is quite obvious, on a little consideration, that as we extend our inquiries, and trace the analogy in different directions, we shall find numberless cases of the most opposite moral character, from the arts of deliberate knavery to the fairest gains of industry and enterprise, all agreeing in this one prominent feature; that the profits of the transaction arose from the superiority of one party to the other in some material knowledge respecting the subject of the contract.

Where then shall we draw the line of fair and unfair, of equal and unequal contracts?

In practice, it is true, the virtuous and benevolent man will find in his own common sense, and in his determination to do unto his neighbours as he would that they should do unto him, much surer guides for his conduct in every situation of life, than any logical or technical rule can afford. Yet the decisions of such a man, in every special case, though they may never be reduced to the forms of reasoning, or carried out into general views, must involve some uniform principle. What then is that principle, which thus admits of such apparently opposite and incongruous applications?

This is by no means a question of pure speculation. It has great and numerous uses. This principle, when clearly settled as a moral rule, will relieve the timidly conscientious from needless scruples; and, what (taking the world as it is,) is of far more importance, it would put an end to that mental sophistry by which men who shrink from deliberate and barefaced knavery, are enabled to argue themselves into a compliance with their secret inclinations, and so cheat themselves out of their own honesty.

If it is of at least equal importance, as furnishing the only sound and satisfactory basis for a just and consistent law of contracts. The slightest inspection of this title of the law as it exists in our own and in most other systems of cultivated jurisprudence, will show that while these different codes contradict one another, they are far from harmonizing throughout with themselves.

All jurists agree in general terms to recognise as the leading principle of the law of contracts, that good faith must be preserved, and that fraud or art on either side, affords sufficient ground for the interference of the law, to protect or relieve the injured party. Follow them out in applying this principle, and the uniformity ceases.

In some cases, like that of the tobacco purchase just stated, legislators and judges, from the apparent necessity of the case, or as chief justice Marshall words, it " from the difficulty of our circumscribing the opposite doctrine within proper limits," have considered the question, not so much on the ground of justice as of policy and convenience, and refused to lend the aid of the law to relieve against unequal contracts, leaving the protection of each man's rights, under such circumstances, to his own prudence and foresight. With regard to the moral regulation of our conduct, they expressly distinguish between the coarse and imperfect morality which they are willing to enforce at their own tribunal, and the sterner decrees of the Interior Forum; —for so the Roman law, by a noble metaphor, has termed the decisions of an enlightened conscience.

Upon the same grounds of necessity and commercial policy, the courts of England, and of the United States have rejected the civil law doctrine of implied warranties, have held that a full price does not imply any warranty of the character of the article, and even that goods of the lowest value may be described and sold as being of the highest, without the unfortunate purchasers having any recourse to the seller, unless he could prove some positive fraud in the transaction:—in short, they have often, in various shapes recognised and applied the harsh maxim of *caveat emptor*, and thrown upon the buyer the burden of every loss against which it was possible for him to have protected himself by caution and suspicion.

But on the other hand, in these same courts, a complete head of commercial law has been gradually filled up almost in our own days, by a continued series of wise judicial legislation, upon principles scarcely reconcileable with these. The law of Insurance requires every where the most perfect sincerity and frankness between the contracting parties, and the slightest suppression of a material fact is held to exonerate the opposite party.

In the same spirit too, the courts of Equity, for the last century, have enforced a very high-toned and almost scrupulous morality in a large class of cases of another sort; invalidating or refusing to enforce agreements, and setting aside or rectifying conveyances made for an inadequate consideration, or through mistake as to facts, or from ignorance of legal rights.

Our systems of equity, and of insurance law, are doubtless indebted, in a great degree, to the influence of the civil code, for this infusion of a different spirit from that which reigned in the ancient common law of England.

The Roman law, as taught by the continental jurists, insisted upon a rigid equality between the contracting parties, and a full and perfect equivalent given and received, in every sale; while it prohibited all reservation concerning any point which the party with whom we contract has an interest in knowing, touching the thing which is the subject of the bargain. This it carries in theory to an extent which few men of business in our days, not excepting the most scrupulously honest, would allow to be wise and just. In many cases, indeed, it must have been literally impossible to apply the theory to practice. It was a natural consequence of this, that both in the Roman law itself, and in those systems of jurisprudence professedly modelled upon it, these principles, after having been broadly laid down as the undoubted and universal moral rule, are restricted for legal purposes by regulations and limitations wholly arbitrary, and somewhat contradictory to the professed spirit of the law.

Such are some of the difficulties and contradictions which appear to embarrass the question of the *nature and degree of equality required in contracts of mutual interest*, as well in reference to *inadequacy of price*, as to the more perplexing difficulty of *inequality of knowledge*.

It is my design, in this essay, to investigate this subject, and to inquire whether its various cases may not all be resolved into a few fixed and broad rules, founded in nature, conscience, and reason.

If this end can be accomplished, I have no doubt that these rules would be of the widest application; would be fitted alike for the guidance of private conscience, and the direction of public justice; would be in unison with the great laws of universal jurisprudence; and not inconsistent with the habits, wants, and true policy of an enlightened age and a commercial country.

CHAPTER II.

Doctrine of the Courts of Common Law and Equity in England and the United States, on Concealment, Inadequacy of Price, Warranty, Secret Defects, Fraud, Scienter—the law of Insurance—Contradictions between the parts of the same system, and the difficulty of assigning a probable reason for them.

THE subject of our inquiry enters so extensively into the pursuits and business of active life, that the law of every civilized country must furnish many rules and decisions in relation to it. At the same time, the circumstances of the various cases in which this question of equality in contracts may arise, are so widely different, and so materially affect the relations of the parties, that it is not always easy to separate the influence of other considerations in fixing a rule of law, or in deciding a case, from the governing principle itself. In our own, and the English jurisprudence, this difficulty, common to all systems, is increased by frequent struggles between reverence for ancient precedent, joined with a prudent fear of rendering the law uncertain and capricious, against the innovations of bolder modern judges, who have eagerly seized the opportunity of new circumstances to bend general rules to the special equity of the case; or who, in those insulated branches of law, which were unoccupied by former decisions, were willing to overlook the analogy of their own system, and to introduce new principles, from some wiser or more politic legislation.

Without entering into any very minute detail or analysis of cases and authorities, let us take a rapid view of some of the prominent points which have been deliberately settled in the courts of England, and of these States, in relation to this head of the doctrine of contracts.

The decision of the Supreme Court of the United States, in the remarkable case of Laidlow v. Organ, above cited, establishing the broad principle that silence with regard to "intelligence of external circumstances, which might influence the price of the commodity, and which was exclusively within the knowledge of the vendee," does not affect the validity of the contract, and that a party in possession of such information is not bound to communicate it, has been for several years acquiesced in as settled law, throughout this country. I do not find in the English reported cases, any precisely similar, or which positively recognise the doctrine to the same extent. But it is strongly confirmed by the utter absence of all contrary authority; especially as in a commercial country, like England, full of enterprise and speculation, the fluctuation of prices from external circumstances operating powerfully and instantaneously upon the market, is an event of every day's occurrence. Had the general opinion of the English bar not been in accordance with the decision of the Supreme Court here, the rapid fluctuations of trade within these last thirty years, which have been caused by the war of the French revolution, the conquests and overthrow of Napoleon, the struggles of South America for independence, the war between the United States and Great Britain, the transition from a state of profuse war expenditure to one of peace and economy, the influence of a depreciated paper currency, and again the change of prices by the return to specie payments, with so many other events, of the deepest interest, could not have failed to have brought into the courts of Westminster Hall numerous suits, in which the unfortunate buyer or seller of goods or stocks would have sought relief from the consequences of some ill-judged bargain made with one of those whose superior political information, extensive correspondence, and weight of capital, gave them the control of the money-market, or of that of the great articles of foreign commerce.

It may be inferred too, from the prevailing spirit of the English law, in which *caveat emptor* is laid down as the general maxim, and every exception or deviation from it, requires some special reason and authority, that the English courts agree with ours in this point. The absence of such authority for an exception, is sufficient proof that the general law is held to apply rigorously.

It may also be strongly inferred from the character, and often from the very language of the equity decisions, in which, while some Chancellors have carried their powers much farther than seemed either wise or just to others as eminent as themselves, all have uniformly stopped short of these bounds. In the gradual extension of the English equity system, since Lord Hardwicke took his seat in Chancery, that court has granted relief in a large class of contracts, by either directly cancelling or refusing to enforce agreements made according to all the forms of law; and this, not only on the ground of positive fraud, but on that of advantages taken from the situation of the parties, or from the ignorance of one coupled with the confidence necessarily reposed in the other, or on account of the mistake of legal right, and the legal import of the terms of the agreement.

But no Equity Judge has yet gone so far as to rescind a contract where, there being no false assertion or artifice, and no breach of trust, the parties differed only in their knowledge of the true present value of the thing bought and sold. With regard to inadequacy of price, it is expressly held that that alone furnishes no ground on which law or equity can rescind an executed contract of sale; and this, says a commentator of authority, "because the law of England has never fixed any certain proportion that the price should bear to the thing purchased."*

The English doctrine, on the effect of inadequacy of price upon executed agreements, has been adopted and confirmed by the highest American authorities.

"I have examined the authorities on this point," says Chancellor Kent, "and am satisfied that it is "not of itself, and *ought not* to be a justifiable cause "of interference, unless the inadequacy be so gross "as to be evidence of *actual fraud*. There is no case "where mere inadequacy of price, independent of "other circumstances, has been held sufficient to set "aside a sale made between parties standing on "equal ground and dealing with each other without any imposition or suppression." After noticing the distinction which has been made between the ground for rescinding a contract and that of decreeing or refusing a specific performance, the learned Chancellor adds, "I need not multiply cases on this point. "The doctrine is settled, that in setting aside con-

* Powell on Contracts, 152. and see cases there cited.

"tracts on account of inadequate consideration, "the ground is fraud, arising from gross inequality." "'Unless the inadequacy does of itself *ex evidentiâ* "*rerum* prove fraud, the rule is,' says Chief Baron "Macdonald, 'that inadequacy has not the weight "suggested.'"*

This cause was afterwards carried up to the Court of Errors of New-York, where the Chancellor's decree was affirmed, and his doctrine expressly recognised. "There is no doubt," said Mr. Justice Platt, "that inadequacy of price is no ground to set "aside a conveyance."†

Thus far the law is clear, and whether it may be thought wise or not, is consistent. But in pushing the same principle a little farther, confusion and uncertainty begin to appear.

The distinction taken by the law, between what it requires to relieve against a complete and perfected contract, and what will be sufficient ground to protect against the execution of it if it were unexecuted, has been transiently noticed. It is very familiar to the English lawyer, but must, I think, be somewhat puzzling to any one whose mind is not familiarized to the nice distinctions of Westminster-Hall. Clearly settled as it is, that he who has made a bad bargain and completed it by the execution of the conveyance, or the transfer of the stock, as the

* Osgood *v.* Franklin, 2 Johns. N. York Chanc. Rep. 24.
† Franklin *v.* Osgood, in Error, 16 Johns. Rep. 558.

case may be, has no remedy unless he can impeach the other party of an actual or constructive fraud; it is far from being settled either here or in England, whether, all other circumstances being the same, if in the interval between the contract and its execution he changes his mind, he can be compelled to stand by his bargain.

On this point, the Courts have administered their equity upon diametrically opposite principles.

The legal reader will find the whole train of English and American authorities, collected with the greatest diligence, and commented upon with much ingenuity and ability, by several distinguished judges and counsel, in the case of Seymour *v.* Delancy,* in the courts of New-York.

On both sides there are strong and numerous authorities, which, as usual, each side explains away, as resting on particular circumstances and not involving any legal principle. Chancellor Kent is, as he always is, learned, lucid, and elegant; and the counsel upon whose argument his judgement was reversed in the court above, are in no common degree able and ingenious. But the reader who is sufficiently skeptical, to doubt the absolute infallibility of great Judges, will smile incredulously over the vain attempts of the Chancellor and the counsel to reconcile in any way, the irreconcileable anti-

* Seymour *v.* Delancy. In Chancery, 6 Johnson's Ch. Cases, 223 to 235, and the same in Error. 3 Cowen, Rep. 445 to 535.

nomies of this branch of English equity. It would not comport with the plan of this essay to enter into the detail of clashing authorities. It is sufficient to say that Chancellor Kent decided in the court below, that "bare inadequacy of price may of "itself, and without fraud or other ingredient, be suf-"ficient to stay the application of the power of the "court to enforce a performance of a private con-"tract;" and that he grounds this opinion upon the decisions or *dicta* of many of the most eminent judges who have presided in Equity. Among those who are claimed as sanctioning his doctrine, are to be found the names of Lords Somers, Hardwicke. Alvanley, and Roslyn, and chief baron Eyre, in England. In America, Chancellor Kent's own high authority is backed by that of the equity court of South Carolina, and of the late venerable and learned Chief Justice Reeve, of Connecticut. On the other hand, the highest tribunal of the state of New-York has determined, that where a contract has been fairly and deliberately made, no inadequacy in it is a sufficient objection to its validity to authorize Chancery to refuse to compel its performance. This doctrine corresponds with the weighty and recent English decisions of Lord Thurlow, Sir William Grant, and Lord Eldon.

Whether under these circumstances Chancery opens its door or not to the party who is desirous to complete his bargain, he has at any rate his remedy at common law, where he may recover damages, for breach of contract. It is, then, important for our inquiry to know what is here the rule of damages. Must the jury give the plaintiff the full amount of what his profits would have been had the sale been perfected? Or, may they take into mature consideration the inequality of compensation, consider the contract as opened, and assess mitigated damages according to their view of the worth of the property or goods?

Here elementary books are silent, and the few cases contradictory. It is settled that if a person agree to take real property, or any thing else, at a given price, on a certain day, and is not ready to receive it and pay for it, the vendor may set it up at auction, sell it for what it will bring, and then in an action recover the difference between the price at this sale, and that of the first contract.* From this it would follow, that the rule of damages is not the actual loss sustained, but the loss of that which might have been gained; and this I should look upon as the unquestionable rule, both from the analogy of the law, and from what I understand to be the usage of our courts, were it not for some as weighty authority the other way. "If "equity act at all, (says Chancellor Kent, in sup-

* Sands & Crump *v.* Taylor & Lovett. 5 Johnson's Rep. 395.—This is also given by Espinasse, as the English rule, in his popular work on the law of Nisi Prius.

port of his opinion that inadequacy of price is a sufficient ground to decline enforcing a contract,) "it must act *ex rigore*, and carry the contract into "execution with unmitigated severity. Whereas, "if the party be sent to law to submit his case to a "jury, relief can be afforded in damages with a "moderation agreeable to equity and good con- "science, and where the claims and pretensions of "each party can be duly attended to, and be admit- "ted to govern the assessment."*

If this be the law, (as in the practical discretion of juries it very probably is in effect,) this head of our jurisprudence, differing as it does so widely, under various circumstances, and in different courts, will afford us but little aid in extracting a general and luminous rule of conduct or of justice.

The comparison of these conflicting decisions and anomalous rules, in this part of our own and the English Equity, almost make us doubt whether the improvements or innovations of modern times have not rather increased than diminished the uncertainty of which Selden complained two centuries ago. Equity, said that learned and bold spoken old lawyer, is what every man chooses to make it. "Sometimes they go according to conscience, "sometimes according to law, and sometimes ac- "cording to rule of court."†

* 6 Johnson's Chan. Cases. 262. † Selden's Tabletalk.

But Chancery law has frequently gone still farther, in recognising the principle that the hardship of a bargain, though resulting from inequality of knowledge between the parties, is no good reason for legal interference.

Some of the latest legal writers lay it down as clear, that where a bargain is merely that the purchaser shall give a certain price for the property sold, unaccompanied with any stipulation express or implied, that he is not to have it for less than its value, the knowledge by the vendee of a circumstance materially enhancing the value of the property, and the known ignorance of it by the vendor, will not affect the validity of the contract.* The doctrine of Lord Thurlow, on this head, seems to agree with that of Chief Justice Marshall:—"Suppose, says he, that A, knowing there to be a "mine on the estate of B, of which he knows B "to be ignorant, should enter into a contract to pur-"chase the estate of B, for the price of the estate, "without considering the mine, the court would not "set aside the contract; because *the buyer was not* "*bound from the nature of the contract to make* "*discovery.*"†

This, it is true, is said argumentatively, and is not a distinct point substantially decided on its own

* Newland on Contracts. Chap. xxviii. p. 434.

† Vide Fox *v.* Mackreth. 2 Brown C. C. 420.

ground. But it is an opinion pronounced broadly and strongly by a judge who had too clear an intellect, and too little ambition of display, to suffer him to throw out his *obiter dicta* at random, or to be tempted to doubtful speculation unnecessary to his argument.

The common law doctrine of Warranty, is in conformity with the prevailing spirit of the decisions we have just noticed. The harsh, but its professors say wise, policy, of the ancient English law, in contradiction to that of the whole of commercial Europe, imposed upon every buyer the necessity of strict caution and vigilance, compelling him to abide the loss of every imprudent or unlucky purchase, unless the goodness and worth of the article was expressly and formally warranted by the seller, or he had knowingly made use of some false allegation, or some art calculated to conceal or deceive. The uniformity of the law of sales was a little disturbed, about the middle of the last century, by an opinion which having been silently introduced by the customs of trade, was supported by respectable authority, and sometimes entertained by the courts. It was held that a *fair price*, or a price at the usual market value of such a commodity, implied a warranty of its soundness, because, it was said, that in the contract of sale, no man could be expected to part with his money without any adequate compensation.* But soon after, a series of very marked decisions, during the most enlightened and liberal period of the English Bench,† restored the rule of the common law as it stood in the days of Fitzherbert and Croke.‡ This has not only been deliberately recognised as law by the Supreme Court of New-York, but carried by them to its greatest extent, in a long and uniform train of decisions.|| It has besides been at different times confirmed and acknowledged by almost all the courts of the United States, which allow the authority of the Common Law.§ The only exception which I know is that of the very able and learned Bench of South Carolina, who have adopted the rule, that a sound price warrants a sound commodity.¶

The seller of personal property is, by his act of sale, considered in law as warranting that he has a right to sell, and that the title is good; but beyond

* Woodison's Lectures, 415. Professor Woodison does not cite any judicial decisions in aid of his own opinion, but it seems to have been often so ruled at Nisi Prius, in his day.

† Douglas, 655. Ib. 18. 2 East, 314. Ib. 446. 3 Durnford & East, 57.

‡ Fitzherbert, N. B. 94. Cro. Jac. 4. Chandler *v.* Lopus. Id. 197. 2d Lord Raymond, 1121.

|| 2 Caines, 48. See also 1 Johnson R. 96, 129, and 274. 4 Johns. R. 421. 5 Johns. R. 354 and 395, &c. &c.

§ 1 Dallas, 217. 4 Dall. 434. 1 Binney 27, in Pennsylvania. 4 Conn. 822. Dean *v.* Mann, in Connecticut.

¶ Whitfield *v.* McLeod. 2 Bay, S. C. R. 380.

this, in all ordinary transactions of buying and selling, the maxim of *Caveat Emptor* is fully established. No matter how defective may be the article sold, for which the full market price of a good commodity has been paid; no matter how much its value may be inferior to its cost; though the wine bought as good, may be sour; though the horse paid for at the highest rate may be foundered; if no fraud or intentional falsehood have been used, the buyer has no remedy. If he cannot rely upon his own judgment in the matter, or upon the good faith of the vendor, it is his business to ask for an express warranty. If he omits this, he takes the risk upon himself.

It is a corollary from this position, that even erroneous representations or descriptions of the quality of the commodity, if made ignorantly,—or to speak more accurately as to the practical operation of the rule, if the buyer cannot prove that they were wilfully false,—impose no obligation upon the seller that the goods correspond with this description. Nay, farther, it has repeatedly been adjudged that even a description of the nature and kind of the thing sold has no effect. So that when certain wood which was bought at a high price under the description of a valuable die-wood much prized in commerce and the arts, turned out to be but logs of a common and wholly different species, fit only for fuel—and when certain cotton goods described as being of a well known fabric of one part of India, were found after the sale to be of a wholly different kind, size, and quality, and manufactured in another quarter of the east—both these were adjudged to be valid and well executed sales.*

The use of falsehood, or of any trick to conceal an intrinsic defect, is universally allowed to be a fraud which furnishes cause for legal relief.

But there is yet another relation in which parties may stand to each other, more closely analogous to that of the New-Orleans tobacco purchase. The wares are bought at the current price, the buyer presuming them to be such as usually at the time bear that price, the seller knowing many important defects.

Now the books and adjudged cases agree that the not disclosing that which could be discovered by reasonable caution and knowledge, will not constitute a fraud, or vitiate a sale, although well known at the time to the seller. If the purchaser be wanting in attention to those points where attention and ordinary knowledge of the matter would

* Seixas *v.* Woods. 2 Caines, 48; and Snell, Stagg, & Co. *v.* Moses. 1 Johnson, 98. This is well settled in New-York, these cases having been followed by many more. Yet with all respect to the very able men who have at different times presided in these courts, I cannot bring myself to believe that this is law in Westminster-Hall, as it certainly is not in some states of this union.

have protected him from surprise or imposition, the maxim *Caveat Emptor* ought to apply.*

But whether or no the vendor is bound by the common law to communicate those latent defects which are not accessible to the buyer, and which he could not by any attention whatever have discovered, is, I think, by no means so clear. I am aware that the common opinion is, that the vendor is so bound. This is stated by Fonblanque as well as by some elementary writers far inferior to him in value and reputation, and it is countenanced by several Nisi Prius cases, and many slight *obiter dicta* of judges.†

But some of the cases cited in support of this rule, are of positive concealment, not of naked silence; others again have been overruled, or doubted after argument;‡ and the language of the old books, and

* Fonblanque, Equity, 380. Espinasse, N. Y. edit. 2, 258. See too 1 Salkeld, 211. 2 Day, 128. &c.

† As in England before Lord Kenyon, at Nisi Prius. Peake, 115, and in Pennsylvania, by Judge Yates. 3 Yates, 862.

‡ As that before Kenyon, (Peake 115,) by Ch. J. Ellenborough, in 3 Campbell, 154, approved by the Court of Common Pleas, in 4 Taunton, 779. The leading American cases cited to this point, in our books, are of false affirmation, or artifice, not silence, and do not apply; or rather prove the contrary. Where the plaintiff had bought at auction some boxes of raisins, which were found to contain rubbish, it appeared that the raisins had been repacked, and at auction were so arranged that the boxes full of good raisins should be on top, the bad boxes beneath.—Hoffman, Recorder, charged the jury, that if they believed the arrangement was designed to conceal the true state of the under boxes, and to impose on purchasers, they should find for the plaintiff, which was done. This is sound law, and good authority; but not for the point for which the American editor of Espinasse cites it.

of the most eminent common law judges of England, in settling other points relating to express or implied warranty, seems decidedly to exclude this distinction, and to agree with Blackstone, who says—"With regard to the goodness of the wares, the vendee is not bound to answer, unless he expressly warrants them, or unless he knew them to be otherwise, and hath used any art to disguise them, or, unless they turn out to be different from what he represented them to the buyer."*

Above all, while the law in such a variety of cases adheres to the doctrine of *Caveat Emptor*, and constantly refuses to admit inadequacy of compensation as a ground of relief against a perfected sale, I can find no express adjudication upon solemn argument, in the English law courts, by which the bare suppression of intrinsic circumstances affecting price is made an exception to this favourite and general policy.

I am, therefore, inclined to believe that the present doctrine has been silently introduced from its apparent fairness and conscientiousness, in the same way as that of implied warranties was some fifty years ago, and that like that, when the question is distinctly brought up, if it should be before a court, anxious to preserve the authority and uniformity of

* 2 Bl. Comm. 451. This passage has been repeatedly cited at length, in the American courts, as containing the accurate rule of warranties. See for instance, Defreeze *v.* Trumper, 1 Johns. Rep. 275.

the common law, and desirous *stare super antiquas vias*, it will be decidedly rejected.

If so, the law as to the suppression of intrinsic and of extrinsic circumstances, will coincide; and it is not easy to say why they should differ. If the more modern be the victorious doctrine, there will then be a direct contradiction of decisions in two very similar classes of cases.

But, at any rate, it must be remembered, that practically the difference is comparatively small; since the burden of proof of the *Scienter*, (or knowledge of defects,) rests upon the plaintiff, and the cases must be rare where the man who thought fit to take the advantage itself, could not, without the help of trick or of perjury, guard himself against the risk of such knowledge being proved upon him.

Though the seller of goods is thus protected from answering for the defects of his unwarranted wares, either by the positive provisions of the law, or indirectly, but as effectually, by its mode of administration; the mechanic or artizan who works by contract or for wages is in a different situation. He who undertakes, for a certain sum of money, to build a ship, or a house, or to make a coat, or to bind a book, is held bound to do his work in a reasonable and workmanlike manner, so that it may have no gross unfitness for the purposes to which it is designed. If the house falls down of itself, or the coat is not wearable, the mechanic loses his claim for the compensation agreed upon; because, say the judges, if there has been no beneficial service, there should be no pay. There has been the greatest uncertainty, it is true, and much positive contradiction as to the legal mode of enforcing this rule. It is doubtful whether the proving that the work was done in a slight and unsufficient manner is a good defence against the demands of the workman, or whether the employer can only resort to a separate or cross action for damages.* But on the main point it is settled, that where a person is employed to do or perform some particular work or business for hire, the law implies that the person so engaged, not only undertakes to do the work, &c. but also to use all due diligence, attention, and skill, in the execution thereof; if he does not, he is liable to the buyer for the amount of damages he may sustain. Thus, though there is no implied warranty of good workmanship imposed on the seller of the finished article, there is upon the mechanic who makes it.

If I order a pair of boots, at the usual price of well-made, substantial boots, and my shoemaker makes me a pair evidently inferior in workmanship and durability, I can compell him to make a proper deduction in his charge, or, according to circumstances, refuse to take them. If I buy the same pair

* 7th East, 479. Peak's Cases, 193, and 15 Johns. Rep. 237, with the English Cases stated in the valuable Note of the Reporter. For the general Rule of Law, Comyn on Contracts, chap. xii. "Of Contracts for Services and Work."

ready made out of the shop of the same man, so he used no false assertion, I must be content with my bad bargain.

This is on a small scale. We may take another example from the noblest of all manufactures, that of ships.

A merchant makes an agreement for the building of a ship. The builder from negligence, (we put all dishonesty out of the question,) executes his contract very badly, with respect to the mechanical part. Here the employer was not wholly obliged to rely upon the builder, for it was possible for him to have examined the work himself as it advanced, and objected to obvious defects ; still the builder is liable for the consequences of his ignorance or carelessness. Not so if he builds and sells on his own account. The law then calls him no longer a workman, but a vendor, and under that name if he sells the same ship at the same price, in good faith, (which he may well do, as we are supposing a case of defects from negligence, or reliance on some under agent,) he is no longer answerable for the faults which he does not positively know or warrant against.

Let us now see how far the analogy of these principles and decisions has been preserved under different external relations, in other titles of the law.

Our law of Insurance, every one knows, is of modern growth. Although the practice of marine insurance had been long in use among merchants, and many of its rules had been fixed by the wise ordinances of the sovereigns, or, the learned labours of the jurists of the continent of Europe; it was not until the time of lord Mansfield that it formed any part of the regular studies of the English lawyer. The liberal learning, and powerful mind of Mansfield, in the course of his long and brilliant career, laid the broad and solid foundations of a system, to which succeeding judges, in Europe and America, have done little more than to fill up and enlarge. Almost every case which came before him presented a new question, with respect to which, the books of the common law could furnish no binding precedent. Thus, in his decisions he was left free to follow the authorities, or to be guided by the reasonings, of the foreign authors; or else to make the judgments of the law correspond with the actual practice of intelligent merchants, and with those universal usages, founded partly in convenience, and partly in natural equity, which might be considered as the common commercial and maritime law of the civilized world.

Hence it is that, though there may be no positive contradiction, there is but little analogy between the law of insurance and the more anciently settled parts of the English law of contracts.

In every contract of insurance the law prescribes to each party, not simply strict integrity, but unreserved frankness and candour. The insured being the party from whom, in most cases, the underwriter obtains the special facts upon which the calculation of the risk is settled; every step of his conduct is watched by the courts with a jealous eye. Every fact within his knowledge, regarding which ignorance or mistake might possibly induce the underwriter to compute his risk upon an incorrect basis, or to enter into the contract on less favourable terms than he would otherwise have insisted upon, is considered in law as a *material* fact, and misrepresentation or suppression of it avoids the policy. So rigidly is this doctrine enforced, that we find the reports full of such *dicta* as these. "This policy "was affected by misrepresentation arising from the "plaintiff's agent. Now, whether this happened "by fraud or negligence it makes no difference, for "in either case the policy is void."* This is said by by Lord Mansfield, in a formal opinion, in which his associates on the bench concur.

Again, by the same, at Nisi Prius: "In all in-"surances it is essential to the contract, that the "insured should represent the true state of the "ship, to the best of his knowledge. On that in-"formation, the underwriters engage. If he state "that as a *fact*, which he does not know to be true, "but only believes it, this is a misrepresentation. "He is bound to tell the underwriters *truth*."†

* Fitzherbert *v.* Mather. 1 Term Rep. 12

† Park. Ins. 182

Not only those points of the agreement which enter formally into the contract, and are acknowledged to be part of the terms of the insurance, by being incorporated into the written policy, but also those collateral statements, either written or verbal, which relate to it, fall within this broad requisition. The underwriter is thus presumed to have computed his premium, and taken the risk, in the reliance that the insured being fully informed respecting all the essential facts, has kept back nothing from him which it is essential for him to know.

If he designedly conceals such a fact, this is regarded by the law as *fraudulent*, in the popular, not the technical, sense of the word, and thus to vitiate the contract on principles of natural justice. But besides what in the view of pure ethicks, might be regarded as a moral fraud; that silence which might be the result of negligence, accident, or inattention, may be as fatal to the claim of the insured. Whatever fact, respecting the state of the ship, the time of her sailing, the nature of her voyage, the last intelligence concerning her, &c. which could possibly influence the mind of the underwriter, in determining whether he would underwrite the policy at all, or at what premium, ought to be explicitly declared, and the want of this so completely puts a bar to the rights of the insured, that the law will afford him no remedy, even for a loss wholly

* 1 Bl. 594. 3 Burrows, 1909.

unconnected with the facts or circumstances concealed or omitted to be told. "The insured," said Lord Mansfield,* "is bound to represent to the underwriters, all the material circumstances relative "to the ship and the voyage. If he did so, though "the omission was by accident or negligence, the "underwriters are not liable. *A fortiori* if he suppressed it from fraud."*

Even doubtful rumours respecting the safety of a ship meant to be insured against past as well as future risks, "lost or not lost," however little credit the owner himself may give to them, ought to be related; and the withholding that information annuls the policy. Thus, where a merchant, on receiving a doubtful account that a ship like one belonging to him, had been taken, caused her to be insured without informing the underwriters of what he had heard, here it was determined that the insurance was void; "for though the insured had no certain intelligence that his ship was taken, yet if he had fairly disclosed what he had heard, it must be supposed that the underwriters would at least have insisted on a higher premium, if they would have insured at all."†

* In Ratcliff *v*. Shoolbred, at Nisi Prius, as reported by Park and Marshall. So too where the omission was from an error in judgment, the insured honestly thinking the matter immaterial. See Shirley *v*. Wilkinson. Douglas, 306, *in note*. Also, Willes *v*. Glover. 4 Bos. and Pul. 14. Ibid. 151.

† Da Costa *v*. Scandaret. 2 P. Williams, 170.

The same frankness is required of the underwriter. If the insurer at the time of underwriting, knew of the safe arrival of the vessel, the contract will be void as to him, and an action will lie for the recovery of the premium paid. Insurance has been well described as a "contract applicable to protect men against any risks which may be of disadvantage to them."* Accordingly, those principles which were originally settled in relation to marine insurance, have been extended to all other contracts of the same sort, such as insuring against fire, robberies, and upon lives, with such modifications only as the special nature of the transaction demanded.

All the rules, thus settled by the English courts, have been universally and explicitly adopted by our American Judges, and are constantly acted upon in our commercial cities. They may be found formally stated and recognised as the law in the Supreme Court of Pennsylvania, by the late Chief Justice Shippen ;† in the Supreme Court of New-York, by Judge Thompson ;‡ in the Court of Errors of the same state, by Chancellor Kent,|| and by Chief Justice Marshall in the Supreme Court of the United States.§

There are, it is true, some few exceptions to these rules, but yet such as rather confirm than lessen the certainty of the leading principle. These relate

* By Judge Lawrence. 2 N. R. 301. † 3 Dallas, 491.
‡ 2 Caines, 58. || 12 Johnson, 514. § 6 Cranch, 274 & 378.

chiefly to intelligence of those public and notorious facts, which are open to all, upon which both parties may exercise their own judgments, and where the only inequality which exists between them is that springing from the difference of natural sagacity, or of commercial and political education and information. On such points, and where from the very nature of the business, a certain degree of secrecy is implied and allowed, either party may be safely and innocently silent.*

The law of insurance is moreover remarkable for another point of contrast to that governing most other mutual contracts. It is this: the very notion of inadequacy of price is wholly unknown to it.—No matter how great the risk taken, and how small the premium; or on the other side, no matter how enormous the premium, and how slight the hazard, if the material facts, so far as known, be fairly communicated, whatever price of the insurance, or premium, is agreed upon, is the adequate price. It would not even occur to an intelligent merchant, or if it did, it would not receive a moment's countenance from the law, that a policy might be rescinded, or the payment of a loss refused, because the premium was inadequate to the chance of loss.

* See the celebrated case of Carter *v.* Boehm. 3 Burrows, 1909: and in general the whole of the 2d section of Chap. X. Book I. Marshall on insurance.

Here let us pause a moment, and observe the difference of that spirit which prevails in the law of insurance from that which regulates the common law regarding other bargains. It is impossible to assign any substantial reason for this remarkable contrast, either upon the grounds of natural equity or upon those of policy. The practice of insurance is, indeed, of admirable utility. Antiquity classed it with the hazards of the gaming table, under the contemptuous appellation of Aleatory contracts. But its modern use which frees trade from the hazards and the spirit of gambling by the application of the principles of gambling itself, is one of the most beautiful inventions of commerce. Yet what is there so sacred in its character or uses, that while in so many other bargains, the courts of common law are content to enforce only that coarse and worldly-minded honesty, which refrains from palpable fraud; here alone they insist upon punctilious honour. Upon what principle of policy can it be, or of common sense, that the law should have selected the body of underwriters, men commonly among the most vigilant and best informed as to their rights and interests, as the special objects of protection from imposition; whilst in such an infinite variety of other contracts and purchases, which the necessities of life compel men of all classes to enter into, and that often blindly and ignorantly, without knowledge of the worth and quality of what they buy, the law's unvarying answer to complaints of fraudulent concealment or unfair advantages, is "*Caveat Emptor;* you should have been more vigilant; if you have been too confiding, or careless, you must abide the loss. It is only to your ignorance and over-confidence in your neighbour's good faith, that the success of that fraud of which you complain, is to be imputed. But it is an old and uncontradicted legal maxim, that *vigilantibus non dormientibus subserviunt leges.*—Therefore, that your ignorance may be punished, that your careless unsuspicious temper may be corrected, and that you may serve as a warning to all others against those faults, the wisdom of our ancestors has decreed that your adversary, who watched while you were asleep, should enjoy unmolested the fruits of his adroitness."

The incongruity of these collateral branches of the law may be made more obvious by the statement of a case or two. They are imaginary indeed, but very probable. In fact they are only so far imaginary as that they bring together in one view, the facts which occur separately every day. We will suppose that a merchant of New-York or Baltimore, extensively engaged in foreign trade, after one of these intervals of contrary winds and long passages which sometimes prevail, and by one of those accidents which have several times happened within our memory, receives the first and only intelligence from Liverpool. His correspondent informs him of a sudden rise of cotton and flour, and the expected short supply of both. A postscript to the same letter adds an account of the loss of a large ship on the coast of Ireland, which from various circumstances of description and date, our merchant has reason to believe, (though not with perfect certainty,) to be his own Charles John. He loses no time to make the best use of his superior intelligence; he sends off his pilot boats to the south to buy up the planter's cotton; and his agents to contract for flour and grain, at the present rates, not only with the regular flour-dealer of the city, who may be on his guard, but with the millers and farmers of the interior. At the same time he effects an insurance on his good ship the Charles John, *lost or not lost*, without giving a hint of the contents of his letter. Now in this latter case, he bargains with the intelligent and skilful officers of an insurance company, men living in the very centre of mercantile and marine news, and with the best information within their reach. In the former case he deals with those, to whom the knowledge upon which he acts, must be wholly inaccessible, and perhaps the very possibility of such intelligence beyond the suspicion of the most vigilant among them. Yet such is our law, that the underwriter, (if these facts can be established,) may confidently stand upon his defence and refuse to settle the loss; while the planter or the farmer has no remedy.

This may serve as one example of intentional advantage. Let us take another of mutual mistake, arising from negligence. A merchant, perhaps less attentive to the details of his business, and the choice of his agents, than a good merchant ought to be, effects an insurance upon the return cargo of a ship of his own, at the time in a foreign port. This he does, without saying a word about the condition and character of the vessel. The next day, believing upon the credit of his captain or agent, that this same ship is staunch and in prime order, he honestly represents her so to be, and sells, or agrees to sell her (we will suppose) to the very merchant with whom in another capacity, as president of a Marine Insurance Company, he had the day before completed his insurance. The cargo is lost or damaged in the voyage, and solely from the defects of the ship; which, upon examination, turns out not to have been seaworthy.

If these two transactions should get into law; in the insurance cause, our president will probably hear the law thus stated, in the words of Marshall and Park: "There is in every insurance, whether on ships or goods, an implied warranty that the ship shall be seaworthy, and fit for the intended voyage. The premium is paid, that the insured may be indemnified against possible loss: but it supposes the insurer may also gain the premium. Now, if the ship be incapable of performing the voyage, the contract on the insurer's part, is without a consideration and void.*" For this law, the authorities are ample and uniform, and judges and insurance lawyers agree that this is clear, upon principles of natural justice.† How great must be the astonishment of our underwriter to learn, that this natural justice, is only justice in an insurance cause; that in his own private affair, the law is quite otherwise. Here he finds that it is settled in England and in New-York, that as "there was no express warranty nor fraud, nor any pretence that the vender knew of these defects, the sale is valid. If there be no warranty, and the vendor sell the ship, such as he believes it to be, the law will not imply that he sold it on any other terms, than what passed in fact."†

In the one case the ship-owner is held to warrant what he said nothing about; the other his express declaration not amounting to a warranty, must go for nothing.

Whatever may be the wiser rule in these cases, it seems wholly unaccountable, that it should not extend to all cases involving the same principle. If

* See Marshall, and all the elementary writers on Insurance, under the head of seaworthiness.

† Parkinson *v.* Lee. 11 East. 314. Snell & Stagg *v.* Moses. 1 Johns. 96. Holden *v.* Davis. 4 Johns. 421.

the law be founded in reason, there ought to be some reason for the difference, and I have searched reporters and elementary writers in vain to find it.

It has, to be sure, been suggested as a sort of excuse for the contradiction, by those who wished to conciliate respect for ancient precedent, with the usefulness of modern improvement, that a perfect frankness is particularly essential to insurance, because the knowledge of the state of the vessel, &c. &c. must be within the reach of the insured, and of him alone, and that the underwriter is of course compelled to rely upon him for all the information necessary to form a calculation of the value of the risk. There is some plausibility, but little soundness in this. In the first place, this reason does not harmonize the law of contracts with itself; for the avowal of important facts and circumstances essential to the true value of the subject of contract, and utterly inaccessible to one party, as we have repeatedly seen, is not held by the law to be of general and universal obligation. Nor is it true, that it is, on the whole, more difficult for an insurer to know the real state of a ship, than for a buyer to learn the actual state and worth of many sorts of commodities. It is indeed, less so than in many instances, as for example in all relating to the mysteries of horse-flesh, or to those of the stock exchange.

If the rule were otherwise than it has been wisely settled, it would be less convenient, indeed, but far from being impossible for a cautious underwriter to require universally such certificates and affidavits of captains, foreign consuls, agents, or inspectors, as would bring the main facts, constituting the risk, very fairly before him, and more perfectly so than actually occurs in half the commercial negotiations of magnitude and complication. Finally, the decisive answer is, that it would be at the underwriter's option to require an express warranty, and thus make any point on which he was at a loss, a condition or part, of the policy. It is not then to this imaginary necessity that this opposition, between the law of insurance and that of sales, is to be attributed, but to different views of policy and of justice, prevailing at different periods, and entertained by judges of different degrees of intellect and expansion.

Within the last eighty years the jurisdiction of Chancery, in England, and more recently in several of the United States, has been gradually extending itself over the most important parts of the law of contracts and sales.

In compelling specific performances of executory agreements where the common law provided merely a remedy in damages, or in refusing to carry them into effect; in controlling the legal operation of conveyances, or other instruments, and interfering so to alter contracts as to make them correspond with the presumed intentions of the parties in opposition to the technical or obvious meaning of the words used; and, finally, in wholly rescinding executed agreements; whilst relief has been given against the rigour or imperfection of the common law, numerous rules have been established which are little in harmony with the general law of bargain and sale. The cases are too numerous, and are too much varied by special circumstances to allow me, within the limits of this brief outline, to make any attempt to give a minute view of this series of decisions. It is sufficient to notice some of those which bear more directly upon our subject. It is settled in equity, that the concealment of material facts, may amount to a degree of unfairness which will shut out the guilty party from all claim for aid to enforce his agreement. Thus, where a tenant who had been long in occupation of lands, obtained an agreement from his landlord for a lease of them; it appeared that the owner had no opportunity of knowing the value of his property, but through the other party, who had already, in anticipation of his lease, underlet the land at a great advance, without risk or trouble to himself. Here Lord Chancellor Macclesfield held, that such an agreement was fraudulent, and, that the court would not aid it by decreeing a performance.*

* Young v. Clark. Prec. Chanc. 538.

Again. Where the estate which the defendant had agreed to buy was represented by the seller as clearing a certain annual rent, (which was literally true,) but no notice was given of the necessary repairs of an embankment to keep out the Thames; it appearing that there had been an industrious concealment of this circumstance during the negotiation; Lord Thurlow considered this as an unconscionable transaction, and dismissed the plaintiff's bill.*

In another class of cases equity has interposed very frequently and decidedly, to set aside releases, or conveyances, made under total ignorance of the party's rights. As where a will had been illegally executed, so that it was, of course, void as to real estate, and the heir at law of the testator ignorant of its legal invalidity, for a trifling consideration, released to the devisee his rights to the estate bequeathed; the release was rescinded.†

Upon the same principle, it has been held, that where a person is ignorant of the real value of the claim, or other unliquidated interest, which he sells, and the bargain is conducted, on the idea of the true value of it being paid, if it be afterwards discovered that a much less value than its worth had been paid, though there be no positive fraud in the affair, equity will relieve against the agreement. Thus, a daughter, ignorant of the real value of her distributive share

* 1 Brown Chanc. C. 440.

† 1 P. Williams, 239.

of her intestate father's estate, or of the mode of ascertaining it, entered into an agreement for the sale of it, and it afterwards appearing that the personal estate amounted to much more than it was estimated at, equity corrected this mistake, expressly because the daughter did not intend to take less than the true value of what she was legally entitled to.*

Another head of equity, bearing no remote analogy to our subject, is to be found in the numerous and well-considered decisions founded mainly upon the consideration of the relative situation of the contracting parties, such as guardian and ward, attorney and client, agent and principal, master and servant. It comprehends all the cases, where from the confidence reposed, and the necessary inequality of the parties in relation to the matters in contract, Courts have looked jealously upon advantages so gained, and in most cases, promptly relieved against them. The doctrine is applied with such rigour in regard to trustees and assignees, that the strict rule seems to be, that the trustee is in no case to be permitted to purchase the trust property for himself, for the reason that his situation giving him opportunities of discovering advantages in the property unknown to others, temptation is held out to keep his knowledge to himself, for his own use.† The wisdom of this, on the first

* 1 Vesey, 400.

† 2 Bro. C. C. 400. 4 Bro. Pa. C. 258.

view too suspicious, rule, is soundly maintained, on the ground of the necessity of preventing the trustee from taking advantage of his superior knowledge by means of concealment, and the impossibility of effectually doing this, except by a rigid prohibition to purchase at all.

"Suppose," said Lord Eldon, "a trustee bought "an estate, and by the knowledge acquired in that "character, discovered a valuable coal mine under "it, and locking this up in his own breast, entered "into a contract with his *cestui qui truste;* if he "chose to deny it, how could the court try it against "that denial?"*

It has been already noticed, that mere inadequacy of price is not allowed, in any of the courts, to be a good ground for setting aside, or relieving against an executed agreement. If a person, say the decisions, with his eyes open, will make a bad bargain, he has no right to complain. Here Equity has again made a distinction. It is laid down, that though an incompetent price does not afford ground in itself for equity to interfere, it may do so, as affording without additional evidence, good proof of fraud. "Fraud," says the great Chancellor Hardwicke, in a luminous and logical arrangement of the several kinds of fraud which fall under the cognizance of the Court of Equity, "fraud may be apparent

* 6 Ves. 627, &c.

"from the intrinsic subject and nature of the bar- "gain itself; being such as no man in his senses, "and not under delusion, would make, on the one "hand, and as no honest or fair man would accept "on the other, which are unequitable and uncon- "scious bargains."* Lord Thurlow recognises the same doctrine, (which, it may be remarked, is not quite uncontradicted,) but after saying, that "there "must be an inequality, so strong, gross, and ma- "nifest, that it must be impossible to state the bar- "gain to a man of common sense, without pro- "ducing an exclamation at the inequality of it," he very characteristically criticises the evident want of precision in his own rule, by adding, "the princi- "ple is loose enough; looser than I wish to be es- "tablished in a court of justice."†

Most of the well-considered decisions in Equity, thus relieving against frauds, so far as they go, inculcate a strict and pure morality, and breathe a rational and manly spirit of honour and frankness. They will, therefore, command the assent of even the unprofessional reader, to their justice as well as to their wisdom.

But the main difficulty is to reconcile these to other parts of the law, and even to other points of

* Earl of Chesterfield *v.* Janssen, 2 Vesey, 155.

† 1 Bro. C. C. 9. Both the principle, and the criticism, are recognised with marked approbation, by a distinguished American Judge, the late W. W. Van-ness, of the Supreme Court of New-York, 7 Johns. Rep. 607

equity jurisprudence. The collision above stated, between great names and long usages, on the question whether inadequacy of price affords ground for refusing to carry into effect unexecuted contracts of sale, is alone sufficient to show how difficult it is to extract from the reports a uniform and clearly defined principle, capable of wide application.

Besides this, it will occur to most men who have ever bought or sold, that a very good bargain on one side, and a very bad one on the other, can but rarely take place by accident. The purchase or sale of a valuable thing, for an insufficient price, must nine times out of ten be caused solely by the fact, that one party knows more in relation to its value than the other. It then remains to inquire, how this refusal to remedy such inequality comports with the relief granted in many other cases of ignorance, or of that constructive fraud which, as we have seen, is frequently no more than the application of superior knowledge of law, or of facts. Since Chancery has gone so far as it has, avowedly upon broad and universal principles of natural ethics, we may naturally ask why, on the same principles, it has not gone further? Moreover, if these are indeed the sound rules of legal ethics, why have not the courts of law assimilated their rules to these; at least so far as their different modes of proof, and powers of granting relief, would allow.

If equity will rescind a contract, for lands obtained at half their value, by an agent or steward, from an indolent or distant landlord, merely by avoiding the giving his employer the information of their true worth; how is it, that in a transaction of trade, the superior information which foreign correspondence, or great industry, gives over the ignorant or indolent as to the worth of any commodities in the market, would not also vitiate the contract?

If a mistake of legal right can claim a remedy from equity, why should not law or equity be bound to remedy the still more important mistakes as to the external relations of peace or war, of foreign demand and domestic supply, which regulate the market price of most commodities?

If, in relation to the law of sales, learned judges hold that a sale of Mediterranean barrilla is fairly executed, by delivering Scotch kelp of a tenth of the value;* how is it the same judges hold in the law of insurance, that a policy extends only to those subjects accurately described in it, so that an insurance upon the raw materials of oil and barrilla, will not cover soap manufactured from them?†

If a great Judge is correct in saying, that "not only good morals, but the common law requires

* The barrilla of commerce and the arts is made from a plant on the Mediterranean coast, and contains about 50 per cent. of alkali, which alone gives its use and value. Kelp is made from sea weeds, in Great Britain, and contains about 5 per cent. of alkali. This is decided in Swett v. Colgate, 20 Johns. Rep. 202.

† Philips on Insurance, 64.

good faith, and that every man in his contracts should act with common honesty, without defrauding his neighbour by false allegations or fraudulent concealments;"* how is it that another great Judge can decide that the "Vendee is not bound to communicate the intelligence of circumstances which might influence the price, but which are exclusively within his own knowledge?"†

If there is a distinction in these and thousands of other similar cases where the law applies widely different rules, where is that line to be drawn? If there is not, and the different parts of the system are clashing and wholly incongruous, which ought to prevail?

If all the parts, so discordant in theory, can harmonize in practice, it must be because one part affords the general rule, the others the exceptions—what then is the general principle, where the deviation? The law of Insurance, and many of the Chancery decisions, claim to be substantially founded upon self-evident propositions of natural justice. The apparent contradictions to natural justice in our civil jurisprudence may then be the result of policy or necessity, where, for wise reason, the law permits what it does not sanction. If this be so, it becomes important for the direction of private conduct, as well as for a discrete application of the

* Per Chief Justice Parsons, 4 Massachusetts Rep. 489.

† Per Chief Justice Marshall, 2 Wheaton, 195.

law, to know what are the respective limits of these antagonizing influences of justice and policy. To all these inquiries, the reported opinions and arguments of the wise and learned men who have presided in our courts, or in those of Westminster-Hall, afford me no satisfactory answer.

We are gravely told, to be sure, that the old common law rules are the sound and wise rules for ordinary use, but that relief is to be granted by equity, on sound discretion, in unreasonable and fraudulent agreements, in unconscionable and hard bargains.*

To this, he who seeks for certainty and precision in the laws of his country, must be constrained to reply, in the strong, but just language of Thurlow; "Rules ought to be fixed, and it would be calamitous "indeed, that the law should rest on such expres-"sions as *hard* and *unconscionable*, which, unless "properly applied, mean little or nothing."†

* See Powell on Contracts. Newland on Contracts, *passim*, and in a noted New-York Chancery Case. 11 Johnson, Ch. C. 231, the Chancellor says, "the general doctrine is that equity will not enforce a hard, or unreasonable, or unequal bargain," &c.

† Adams *v.* Weare. 1 Bro. Ch. C. 568.

CHAPTER III.

The doctrines of the CIVIL LAW, and of the modern systems founded on it, especially the FRENCH CODE, respecting Warranty,—Concealment,—Inadequacy of Price. The speculative opinions of civilians and writers on natural law,—Criticisms and objections.

THE incongruities of our law are more a matter of regret than of surprise. The reason of their existence is to be found in its history. This system of jurisprudence was the slow growth of many ages, and of several centuries. In each successive modification which it underwent, in the progress of civil freedom, in the admixture of foreign learning and law, in its necessary adaptation to the ever augmenting wants of an extensive, bold, and liberal spirited commerce, as new relations and new usages arose, new views of equity or policy were opened, or old rules were adapted to purposes for which they were never intended, by Judges who partook of the altered spirit of the times. In this respect we may anticipate a more satisfactory result from an examination of the Roman law, and of the modern legal institutions founded upon it. These being regularly digested into written codes, settled by authoritative definitions, and commonly reasoned out from first principles, have the method and dignity of science, and the unity of system.

It is the proud boast of the civilians, (to use the language of Chancellor D'Aguesseau, one of the best and wisest of the many great men whose virtues and talents shed a lustre over the magistracy of the old French régime,) "That Justice had "revealed all her mysteries to the Roman jurists. "By their intellectual superiority alone and without "the aid of political power, they have given laws "to the remotest posterity. All nations still con-"sult them, and receive the responses of eternal "truth."

The German Leibnitz, in whom was displayed the rare union of the profoundest mathematical, metaphysical, classical, and legal science, has compared the law of Rome, for precision of language, and closeness of deduction, to the demonstrations of geometry. "Nor, (adds he) are the traces of a re-"fined and deeply meditated system of jurispru-"dence, any where to be found more visible or in "greater abundance. And even in those cases "where its principles are departed from, either in "compliance with the language consecrated by "technical forms, or in consequence of new sta-

"tutes, or of ancient traditions, the conclusions "thus rendered necessary are deduced with the "soundest logic, and with an ingenuity which ex- "cites admiration."* These praises, so far as respects the civil code, are not unmerited. The Roman law, with all that abject submission to arbitrary power,† which disgraced the descendants of the Scipios and the Catos of the republic, rarely permitted its expounders and legislators to rest their decisions upon naked precedent and authority. Its rules were invariably either deduced from the universal principles of natural law, or from the common sentiments, sympathies, and feelings of mankind. Its most solemn and authoritative provisions of distributive justice appeal, one while to natural reason; "*Cum Ratio naturalis quasi lex queedam tacita addiceret,*" &c;‡ Now to humanity and charity: "*Humanum est,*" &c. :|| and on this very subject of good faith and equality in contracts, its constant language is that of conscience and benevolence; "*ex fide bona*" or "*ut inter bonos bene agier opportet.*"

Its theory, if not always true, is ever plausible,

* Leibnitz, as quoted by D. Stewart, Elements 2.

† The avowed political doctrine of the Justinian law, is "*Quod principi placuit legis habet vigorem;*" But it is remarkable that under the weakest and most vicious princes, the seat of justice was filled by the wisdom and integrity of Papinian and Ulpian, and the purest materials of the code and pandects, are inscribed with the names of Carracalla and his ministers. See Gibbon, Dec. and Fall. chap. 44.

‡ Dig. 48; 20, 7, on successions and inheritance.

|| In the law, "*de recindend. vendit.*"

consistent, and beautiful. Its theoretical errors, if it have them, seem to arise chiefly from those false deductions which ingenious men of the closet, by attending more closely to words than things, may by the use of a metaphysical and verbal logic deduce argumentatively from the soundest premises. Its unanswerable eulogy is to be found in the fact that its intrinsic excellence has overcome the prejudices of nations whose earlier institutions had been modelled in other shapes, that it has commanded the assent and reception of the greater part of civilized Europe, and a large portion of America, and that by serving as the surest light to the inquiries of the learned, and the discussions of the diplomatists, it has formed the real basis of public and international law.*

Tu regere imperio populos Romane memento:

Roman! tis thine, with awful sway
To rule mankind, and make the world obey:

was the lofty injunction of Virgil to his countrymen, when he saw the nations of the earth crouching beneath their arms. Rome's military glory has long since passed away. Her civil wisdom retains and enlarges its empire. For the last three or four centuries, Germany, Bohemia, Hungary, Poland, Scotland, France, Italy, Holland, and their colonies, have received its rules, either directly as

* "On the civil law," Sir Wm. Scott somewhere observes, "great part of the law of nations is founded."

common law and legal reason, or indirectly by re-enacting it in their peculiar codes; the illustrations, the reasons, and even the meaning of the terms of which, are to be sought in the Roman law. In our own days, we have seen the definitions, the rules and reasonings of Caius, and Papinian, of Ulpian, Paul, and Tribonian, the jurists of the Roman and the eastern empire, not so much re-enacted as recognised in the recent codes of France and Prussia, and Louisiana.

In the civil law, and in its derivative systems, it is laid down as a universal and fundamental position, that the contract of sale depends wholly upon natural law; not only owing its origin to that law, but being entirely governed by the rules deduced from it.* Upon this solid foundation has been raised a consistent and beautiful system of law in relation to the losses sustained from ignorance of circumstances or facts *intrinsic* to the subject of sale; such, for instance, as secret defects lessening the worth of the thing sold as an object of commerce, or rendering it useless, for the purpose for which it was bought.

It is remarkable, that, on comparison, this will be found to be, in every part, nearly the reverse of the law of England, on the same head.

* Ce contrat est entierement du droit naturel car non seulement il doit à ce droit son origine, mais il se gouverne par les seules regles tirées de ce droit. Pothier, Contrat de Vente.

The civil lawyers say that the seller contracts with the buyer, to convey him the property of the thing sold; and that in the meaning of the parties, this property signifies a useful property. They maintain that there results from the understanding of the agreement alone, and without other stipulation, that obligation, which in the common law is called an implied warranty of quality. They regard it as a necessary incident or consequence of a sale that the seller, (unless he expressly disclaims the responsibility,) should be held to warrant against all defects or injuries which are of a nature to render the thing sold unfit for the ordinary purposes to which it is employed in commerce or manufactures, or for the particular object for which it is known to be purchased.* Those faults to which this warranty extends are termed redhibitory, (*rehibitoriæ* in the Roman, *redhibitoires,* in the Napoleon code;) and are quite as definitely fixed as the nature of the subject will admit, by numerous and precise rules, all exemplifying the same leading principles, and drawn from the highest antiquity of the Roman law. Local usages, and peculiar circumstances, vary the rule as to wine, or horses, or ships, or

* This provision thus re-enacted in the present French code. "Le vendeur est tenu de la Garantie à raison des defauts cachés de la chose vendue, qui la rendent impropre à l'usage auquel on la destine, ou qui diminuent tellement cet usage que l'acheteur ne l'aurait pas acquise, ou n'en aurait donné qu'un moindre prix." Art. 1641.

grain, or houses, or farms; but the comprehensive principle is, that the seller is held to be answerable for all those defects of the thing sold, which unfit it for its common use, or so lessen that usefulness that the buyer would not have purchased, or would have given a less price, if he had known them. These defects, when proved, are sufficient, without bringing the knowledge home to the party, to oblige him either to return the purchase money, or, according to circumstances, to make amends for the difference of value. For this purpose, were provided a form of action, the *Actio Redhibitoria,* for the rescinding the contract, and that *Quanto minoris* for damages. Between parties mutually ignorant and innocent, the Roman law went no farther. It was content that every thing should be restored to such a state as if no sale had taken place: "*omnia in integrum restituantur perinde ac si neque venditio intercesserit.*" The modern French code expressly gives the buyer the choice to keep his purchase and to receive the estimated difference, or to give back his bargain, and receive his payment for it.*

But whenever the knowledge of such defects can be brought home to the vendor, or if from his peculiar situation or business there is just reason to presume it, he is then held to respond in damages not only for the full value of the sound commodity,

* Code Civile, art. 1644.

but for interest and all consequential or indirect injuries, inconveniences, and losses.

Thus, for example, if a farmer sell cattle, knowing them to be infected with a contagious distemper, and conceals this fact, such concealment is held to be a fraud, which renders him responsible, in addition to the difference of price between healthy and sick cattle, also for the loss of any other cattle to which the disease might be communicated.*

This too is the modern law of the continent of Europe. "If the vendor, (says the civil code of France,) knew the faults of what he sold, he is held in addition to the price which he has received, to be answerable for all damages and interest accruing. If he were ignorant, he is held only answerable to make good the price."†

In short, all the rules and decisions of the ancient Roman law on this subject have been implicitly received wherever the civil law has had any positive authority. Nor, setting aside all consideration of their justice, is it a slight proof of their practical utility, that after the long and varied ex-

* See Pothier on Obligations, 165. The rule of law is thus illustrated and exemplified in the Digest, 19, 1, 13. Inter eum, qui sciens quid aut ignorans vendidit, differentiam facit in condemnatione ex empto; ait enim qui pecus morbosum, aut lignum vitiosum vendidit, siquidem ignorans fecit, id tantum ex empto actione præstaturum, quanto minoris essem empturus, si id ita esse scissem; si vero sciens reticuit et emptorem decipit, omnia detrimenta, quæ ex ea emptione emptor traxerit, præstaturum ei; sive igitur ædes vitio ligni corruerunt, ædium estimationem, sive pecora contagione morbosi pecoris perierunt quod interfuit idoneé venisse erit præstandum.

† Civil Code, art. 1645, 1646

perience of the French jurisprudence, these principles, almost in the very form in which they were arranged and methodised by Pothier, nearly an hundred years ago, were, in the beginning of the present century, embodied in that code which is the noblest monument of the fame and genius of Napoleon.

Let us now see what are the consequences which the doctors of the civil law deduce from the same or similar principles, in relation to those cases where the loss of either party arises not from intrinsic defects, but from the ignorance of *extrinsic* circumstances, known to the one party and not accessible to the other.

The civilians hold that in all contracts the observation of that good faith between the parties which natural justice and conscience would approve, is of the very essence of the transaction.—Their grand maxim is, that good faith is essential to all bargains. "*Bona fides in omnibus contractibus necessaria.*" In discussing the questions which arise out of this principle, Pothier thus states the doctrine of the civil law regarding the advantages which may be gained by concealment and reservation. "In all contracts of mutual interest, "good faith not only forbids falsehood, but also *all* "*concealment of every thing which he, with whom* "*we bargain, has an interest in knowing, in rela-* "*tion to the matter which is the subject of contract.*

"The reason of this is, that justice in these con-
"tracts consists in equality: every thing then that
"tends to infringe this equality, is against equity.
"It is evident that any reservation on the part of
"one of the contracting parties, respecting any
"thing which the other may have an interest in
"knowing, violates this equality; for as soon as
"one party has a knowledge of the matter supe-
"rior to that of the other, he has an advantage in
"forming his bargain. He understands what he
"is doing better than the other, and of course the
"equality between them is at an end. In applying
"this doctrine to the contract of sale, it follows
"that the seller must disclose every circumstance
"within his knowledge respecting the matter which
"the buyer has an interest in knowing, and that he
"sins against that good faith, which should reign
"in this contract if he conceals any such circum-
"stance.

"This is the doctrine of Florentinus in the law
"43, 2 *Dig. De cont. empt. Dolum malum a se
"abesse præstare venditor debet, qui non tantum
"in eo est qui fallendi causâ obscure loquitur, sed
"etiam qui insidiose, obscure dissimulat.*"

"According to these principles, the vendor is
"obliged not to conceal any of the defects of the
"thing sold which he knows of, although these
"defects should not be of that kind concern-
"ing which the civil law requires an implied

" warranty, but even such defects as the vendee " would not be suffered to complain of, if the ven- " dor had been wholly ignorant of them. This rule " must hold good, even where the vendor who con- " cealed the faults of his wares, did not sell them " for more than they were were worth. This is " because that he who sells me any thing has no " right to make me pay the highest price for it un- " less I consented to take it at that rate. He ought " not to require of me a higher price than that " which I would voluntarily give, nor to practise an " artifice to induce me to buy at a higher rate than " I would have been willing to pay if I had known " the fault which he fraudulently concealed.

" Good faith obliges the seller not only to refrain " from suppressing the intrinsic faults of what he " sells, but universally from concealing any thing " concerning it, which might possibly induce the " buyer not to buy at all, or not to buy at so high a " price. For instance ; the buyer may have his " action, if the seller has concealed the existence " of a bad neighbourhood to a real estate sold by " him, which if it had been known would have hin- " dered the purchase: *Si quis in vendendo prædio " confinem celarerit quem emptor, si audisset, emp- " turus non est.* *Dig. L.* 15, 8.

" These decisions of the Roman jurisconsults, " are more correct and agreeable to justice than " those of Saint Thomas, (Thomas Aquinas) who

" permits the seller to suppress the faults of his " goods, except in two cases. 1. If the fault be of " a nature to cause the buyer some injury. 2. If " the seller availed himself of this reservation in " order to sell at a higher rate than his goods were " worth. This decision is repeated in his " Quod- " libitic questions." It seems to me wrong, since " as the vendor is himself quite free to sell or not to " sell even at a fair price, if that price does not " suit the buyer; it is unjust to lay a snare for this " liberty, which the vendor ought equally to enjoy, " by concealing from him the faults in order to in- " duce him to buy what otherwise he would not " have been willing to purchase at that rate, know- " ing its defects.*"

The same reasoning which prohibits reservation on the part of the buyer, applies of course with equal force, to the seller; and the civil law writers are equally strong in both points.

" Another species of fraud, (says Pothier,) is " when the buyer keeps back from the seller the " knowledge which he has of the thing sold, and " which the seller has not. For example, I know " that the estate which you sell me, and which I am " well acquainted with, and know that you are not, " is let at a low rent, and that at the expiration of " the lease, it may be re-let at a much higher rate; " it will be a fraudulent act to conceal and take ad-

* Pothier, Contrat de Vente, No. 238 et seq.

" vantage of my knowledge of this inadequacy of " the rent. The reason of this is, that the good " faith and equity which ought to govern these con- " tracts, oblige the contracting parties to declare " any thing which they know, affecting the object " of sale. The law 43, 2 *Dig. de contr. empt.* " regards all concealment in this respect as fraud. " It is true that this law literally speaks only of the " vendor, but it applies equally to the vendee ; the " obligations being reciprocal."*

Such is the strict doctrine of the ancient Roman law in reference to reservation respecting *extrinsic* circumstances. It seems thus to have been actually administered in the tribunals of the Roman empire ; and the reason and justice of it are strongly asserted and maintained by the modern civilians of Europe, in their theoretical speculations on the equity of *Synallagmatic*, or mutually obligatory, contracts.

But the history of this doctrine may excite some doubts as to its soundness ; certainly it will as to its policy. Unlike the analogous doctrine of implied warranty as to kind, quality, and soundness, it no longer serves as a practical rule. Thus a very strong presumption that it was carried to an extent impracticable in the business concerns of modern life, arises from the fact that while it preserves

* Pothier. Vente, 295

its rank in the theoretical institutes of the law, it has been silently dropt from modern use. Pothier informs us that this was the case in the countries of the civil law in his day. "Though, (says Pothier,) "it is with regard to the actual administration of "civil justice that the Roman jurisconsults esta-"blished these principles, and though they ought "to be rigidly followed *in foro conscientiæ*, as a "rule of private duty, nevertheless they are little "observed in our courts; and a buyer would not "readily be listened to who should complain of "any concealment or suppression not falling with-"in the rules of warranty of soundness: *("lorsque "le vice n'est pas un vice redhibitore.")* The in-"terests of commerce do not permit parties to "break their bargains, once concluded; they have "only to blame their own negligence in not being "better informed. There are, nevertheless, cer-"tain reservations, as to extrinsic circumstances, "which have claimed the attention of the law, and "which are noticed in the exterior forum. Such "as where the vendor knows the thing he sold "does not belong to him, or that it is not absolute-"ly or completely his, or that it is subject to claims "and encumbrances."*

The present civil code of France, admitting the same theoretical doctrine, impliedly limits it by the

* Pothier de Vente, 238, 239.

same necessity; it declares that "Error is not a "ground of invalidating contracts, except where "it falls upon the substance itself of the thing "which is the object of it."* And again in a subsequent article. "Fraud is a cause of vitiating a "contract when the manœuvres (thus requiring "some special act, beyond mere silence) practised "by one party are such that it is evident that with- "out them the other would not have consented." But "Fraud must be proved, and is never to be "presumed."†

The speculative ethics of the earlier Roman jurisconsults are said, by those who have studied the history, and become most imbued with the spirit of their law, to have been drawn from the Stoic philosophy.‡ Tacitus speaking of a noble Roman

* "L' Erreur n'est une cause de nullité de la convention que lorsque elle tombe sur la substance même de la chose qui en est l'objet." Code Civ. Titre 114, art. 1110.

† "Le Dol est une cause de nullité de la convention, lorsque les *manœuvres pratiqués* par l'une des parties sont telles, qu'il est evident que sans ces manœuvres l'autre partie n'aurait pas contracté.

Il ne se presume pas, et doit etre prouvé.—Art. 1016.

‡ "The jurisprudence which had been grossly adapted to the wants of the earlier Romans, was polished and refined in the seventh century by the alliance of the Grecian philosophy. The Scevolas had been taught by use and experience; but Servius Sulpicius was the first civilian who established his art on a certain and general theory. For the discernment of truth and falsehood, he applied as an infallible rule the logic of Aristotle and the Stoics; reduced particular cases to general principles, and diffused over the shapeless mass the light of order and eloquence. From the Portico, the Roman civilians learnt to live, to reason, and to die; but they imbibed in some degree the prejudices of the sect, their love of paradox, their pertinacious habits of dispute, and a minute attachment to words and verbal distinction." Gibbon, chap. 44. See also Heinescius. Hist. Juris. Roman. et German. §1555, ont he influence of the Stoic philosophy upon the law. "Jurisconsulti plerique Stoici."

whom he evidently delights to portray as his model of civil virtue, says: that he embraced the opinion of those teachers of wisdom who regard that which is honourable as the only good, that which is base as the only evil; who look upon power, wealth, and all other things external to the mind, as things neither evil nor good.* Together with the stern and grand truths of this philosophy, they unquestionably imbibed many of the errors of a doctrine which, however beautiful in speculation or elevating in sentiment, is not in unison with the true nature of man, and claims for him a prouder independence from external things, than his weakness will allow or his duties require. The rules and arguments above cited seem to me to partake of this character, and to be little fitted for the ordinary commerce of life. They may correspond with the sentiments of a jealous and refined personal honour, but they certainly go beyond the limits which strict justice and simple integrity require.

The efficient cause of the practical abandonment of the ancient civil law doctrine of concealment, is unquestionably to be found in its hostility to the policy of modern civilized society. A literal compliance with it, and a rigid interference of the tribunals to enforce its rules, would speedily put

* Illos doctores secutus, qui sola bona quæ honesta, mala tantum quæ turpia: potentiam, nobilitatem, ceteraque extra animum neque bonis neque malis adnumerant; says Tacitus, speaking of Helvidius Priscus

an end to the inestimable advantages, that society derives from the wholesome stimulus to commerce, and the arts, given by the prospect of profit to be acquired by superior skill and industry, by minuter attention to business, or by a more extensive correspondence and more authentic intelligence.

Sound policy is never in collision with sound morality, and the greatest truths of political economy are but those of morality viewed under another aspect. Our subject involves the consideration of the moral as well as the legal question. Let us then look at the reasoning of the civilians as furnishing directions for conscientious dealing, without reference to the wisdom of any legal enforcement of them. Considered then in the light of moral reason alone, this doctrine, which is well meant in intention, and drawn from just notions of right and wrong, is evidently far too broad in its terms, and wanting both in precision and in truth. It is not true that either party is bound in conscience, or even by a delicate and fastidious honour, to communicate to the other "*omne quod interrerit scisse,*" every circumstance regarding the business, which the buyer has an interest in knowing. A thousand examples of familiar occurrence may be imagined where the peculiar talent or the industry of one man has given him a superiority of knowledge which it would be of the greatest use to the other side to participate in, but which no one could ever think him bound to communicate.

The improvements of commerce and navigation every day open new and distant markets to the sagacity and enterprise of the English and American trader. Suppose now, that a merchant has at great expense and risk ascertained that Cochin China, or some unfrequented port in India, offers a most profitable market for some articles in no special demand at home. Is it dishonest in him to make the most of this hardly and dearly earned knowledge, before it becomes common to others? Cannot he honestly purchase his opium, his ginseng, or his bark, at the current rate, without first telling the seller that it would be more for his interest not to sell at the price he offers, but to make a shipment on his own account to the newly discovered market?

An ingenious chymist discovers a certain simple mode of restoring damaged wheat, so as to answer some of its most valuable purposes:—May he not conscientiously go into the corn-market and buy the heated grain for his own immediate profit, at as high a price as the owner could possibly otherwise get for it, without informing the merchant or farmer of his discovery? Yet this it would of course be for the other's interest to know, since it would make his damaged grain almost as valuable as the best.

My mechanical friend has invented a new and cheap mode of working and polishing marble. It is certain that when brought to perfection, and introduced into common use, it will vastly increase the demand for the raw material. Now is there any iniquity in his purchasing a marble quarry in the neighbourhood of some great city, without giving notice to the owner of his invention?

Was there any dishonesty in a moral point of view, in the inventors of the steam, and horse ferry boats, purchasing the exclusive rights of ferriage over the Hudson or other great rivers, at a price, which before these inventions, was considered as ample and liberal?

In all these cases, and in ten thousand like them, the seller has a direct interest in knowing the secret which the buyer justly regards as his own private and peculiar property. Nor is it difficult to suggest as many actual or possible cases, where all men of sense will allow that the seller may as honestly take advantage of the favourable state of the market, without communicating to the buyer any portion of that information which would enable him to obtain his goods at a lower price. Any set of goods particularly suited to the taste or demands of a large class of customers, may be raised for a time to a price paying far more than the usual rate of profit, in consequence of the supply being in the hands of individuals, whose knowledge of some art, or of the mode, or place of obtaining the article at a cheap rate, gives them a partial monopoly. Certainly, such men may very conscientiously profit by their good fortune, or their better knowledge than their competitors, in silence, without being obliged to inform their customers of the high profits they receive, or teaching them how they may supply themselves at a cheaper rate.

Again: If I have a horse to sell for my friend, may not I get as much as he will bring, without communicating to every chapman, that the owner has no longer any use for him—that he is going to Europe, and has determined that if he cannot immediately get his price, he will sell his horse at auction, for what he can get? Yet this too, obviously, might be a fact very much for the buyer's interest to be informed about.

Indeed, upon a literal application of the principles of the digest, and its most celebrated commentator, Pothier, it seems to me that two merchants could never make an honest bargain, for the ordinary objects of commercial speculation, without each of them letting the other into all his plans of trade and views of the changes and future state of the market. Yet a man must be narrow and ignorant indeed, to deny that it is possible to gain wealth, with the most perfect honesty, and even with the most punctilious honour, from the profits of trade, not by accident, but by superior skill; or, in plainer words, that it is possible to make money honestly, by good common sense, joined to better knowledge than others have.

These advantages, on whatever scale they may

occur, from the profits of the fruiterer, who supplies a wealthy city with a few daily baskets of fruit, up to those of the gigantic capitalist who controls the price of the staple commodities of nations, in the great market of the world, are the necessary and lawful stimulants of that activity which, in the search after private profit, opens a thousand springs of prosperity and plenty for the use of all; and within just limits, are as free from moral guilt as they are fruitful of public utility.

For these reasons I cannot agree with Pothier, that the opinion of the elder civilians, whom he follows, should be rigidly adhered to in the tribunal of conscience, although it may not be enforced by the tribunals of human justice.

Still, it must be allowed, that setting legal considerations out of view, it is most certain that there are numerous circumstances under which concealment of what it is for the other party's interest to know, is a fraud. Many cases, where the English Equity interposes, are indisputably of this kind, and there are, I think, many more where it does not.

The fact is, that the civil law, by pushing its notions of morality to an unreasonable extent, has, by a natural consequence, more than defeated its own object; so that, in effect, its remedies against wrong, fall as far short of the true rule of justice, as its theory goes beyond it.

But since most of these points, when they occur individually, do not present great difficulties to the minds of virtuous and intelligent men, it is certainly possible to ascertain what that sober and true rule is, which, without aiming at impracticable and romantic disinterestedness, gives just as little countenance to loose and casuistical dishonesty. Once settle this, and there is no sound reason why the decisions of the courts of law should not, so far as they have the means of ascertaining facts and applying remedies, be the very echo of the voice of that strong master of the soul, "the inexorable judge within."

The paternal care of the Roman code, over the ignorant, the careless, and the credulous, did not end here. It provided a remedy, in cases of "Enormous Lesion," or gross inadequacy of price. Where neither actual deceit, nor the constructive fraud of silence could be proved, it teaches that such gross inadequacy alone, amounts to fraud in the very substance of the contract.*

One of the provisions of the code runs thus: "If you or your father have sold any thing of great value, for a small price, equity requires that you should receive back your property, on paying its value to the purchaser; or, if the buyer so chooses, that he should make good to you its fair value. It may be consi-

* "Dolus re in ipsâ."

dered, as having been sold at too low a rate, if less than half its true value were paid for it."*

This rule has received the praise of speculative politicians and historians; and amongst others, Voltaire, in one of his brilliant but superficial sketches has selected it for the special subject of eulogy, as being an institution doing honour to the enlightened views of the age which gave it birth. But here again the history of the civil law affords a practical comment upon its theory, which suggests suspicions as to the wisdom of this rule.

In the countries governed by the civil law, the necessities of trade soon exempted from its operation all personal property, or as the civilians speak, things moveable, and it was confined in practice to real estate, or rather to lands, by whatever tenure they were held.

" With respect to moveables, (says Pothier,) the " vendor is not allowed by the Courts to set aside a " sale on account alone of the lowness of price; how- " ever enormous the deficiency may be. Our custom " of Orleans has an express regulation on that head, " and this is generally received as law."†

* " Rem majoris pretii, si tu vel pater tuus minoris distraxerit; humanum est ut vel pretium te restituente emptoribus fundnm venumdatum recipias, auctoritate judicis intercedente: vel si emptor elegerit, quod deest justi pretii recipias. Minus autem pretium videtur si nec dimidia pars veri pretii soluta est." Cod. 1, 2. *de rescindenda venditione.* Lord Chancellor Hardwicke seems to have drawn from this source his second class of frauds, " that apparent from the intrinsic nature and subject of the bargain itself;" but with a manifest improvement. See 11 Vesey, 156.

† Pothier Traité de Vente. §303, and more in detail. §339, 340.

It next soon began to be denied, that the buyer, who had paid too much for his land, was entitled to the same equity with the unfortunate vendor. Still, in some shape or other, but every where with some modifications and limitation, this principle, which was distinguished by the singular title of *Equitas Cerebrina*, was widely diffused. But this was not without objection and opposition.—Learned civilians* who, perhaps, passed among their brethren for a kind of legal freethinkers, maintained that the "*Dolus re in ipsa*" was a metaphysical figment of the law, having no existence in the nature of things. They maintained too that the whole doctrine was an interpolation of later jurists, and was unknown to the purer ages of the Roman law; being in direct opposition to other rescripts and passages of weight, which declare that the courts are not to be troubled with litigation, founded on complaints of inequality of compensation, without fraud."†

* Christian Thomassius, a German civilian, has written a dissertation, "De Equitate Cerebrina," on this very subject of inadequacy of price. It is I believe a rare book. I have never seen it, and know it only from some account of it given by M. Berlier, in his learned and powerful, but unsuccessful argument on this head of the French Code in the Discussions of the Council of State. The work of Thomassius is, evidently, of deep research; and I should judge it from M. Berlier's statements to be also, of no common power of original and correct thinking.

† Venditionis atque emptionis fidem nulla circumscriptionis violentiâ factam rumpi, minine decet. Nec enim solâ pretii vilioris querelâ contractûs sine ullâ culpa celebratus litigioso strepitu turbandus est." Cod. 43, *de cont. empt* 2. And again under the very same title with the law of rescision, it is laid down that fraud is to be judged of not by the amount of price, but by the character of the transaction. "Dolus emptoris, qualitate facti, non quantitate pretii æstimatur." Cod. 43, 10.

In the jurisprudence of France, this principle was early confined to real property. During the revolutionary struggles, the uncertainty of the titles of confiscated property, the sales of the national domains, as well as the immense fluctuations in nominal price arising from the depreciation of assignats, and other paper currency rendering it utterly imposssible to be executed, it was expressly repealed. When the Civil Code was formed and promulgated under the auspices of Bonaparte, First Consul, the law of Rescision as to sales of real estate for very inadequate prices was embodied in the Code.*

From the reported discussions upon the Code, in the French Council of State, it appears that this was not without great opposition from distinguished men of the bar, and wholly without the approbation of the judicial tribunals of the nation, to which the rough draft, or *Projèt* of the code, had been submitted. It was supported by the First-Consul himself, by the Second Consul, Cambaceres, and by most of those who formed a part of the ad ministration.† From this, there is reason to think that political considerations, extrinsic to mere equi-

" * Si le vendeur à eté lesé de plus de sept douzièmes dans le prix d'un immeuble, il a le droit de demander la rescision de la vente, quand même il aurait expressement renoncé dans le contrat à la faculte de demander cette rescision, et qu'il aurait declaré donner la plus value." Code Civile, 1674.

† See the "Discussions du Code Civil, dans le Conseil d'Etat." upon the adoption of article 1674. Titre de la Vente.

ty, had their share in this decision. Probably it might have been at that time deemed expedient to give stability to the titles and possessions of landed estate, which had been so much shaken by the revolution; and the solidity of which was so necessary to the contemplated new form of government. Be this as it may; the general principle of the justice or right of rescinding sales, on account of mere inadequacy of price, seems to be formally abandoned in the French code in several ways.

1st. By refusing to grant this relief in all commercial transactions and sales of moveables.

2d. By refusing to extend it to an unequal exchange, even of land or houses, no matter how great the inequality.

3d. By refusing in terms to the buyer, that equity it professes to provide for the seller.

The courts of justice in Saxony, a country governed by the civil law, have always rejected the principle of granting relief for inadequacy of price, unless there are other circumstances indicating fraud.* In the code of Prussia, the rule being in like manner borrowed from the civil law, is yet precisely the reverse of the French code. It denies to the seller of real property, and grants to the buyer, the privilege of relief against a sale for a grossly deficient price†.

* So stated by Thomassius, as quoted by M. Berlier: *Discussions du Code.*

† Not having access to the Prussian code itself, I cannot say whether it extends to personal or moveable property. This is not expressed in M. Berlier's translations of some articles of the Prussian code.

These contradictions with one another and themselves, in systems of law having the same common origin, and professing to be founded on the same process of reasoning, give fair ground to doubt whether there is not some radical error either in the principle or in the manner of enunciating it, unfitting the rule for the purposes of ordinary life, or of distributive justice. The doctrine itself, meanwhile, not only keeps its place speculatively and without limitation, in the books of the civilians, but has been incorporated into the systems of the most distinguished writers on the law of nature and nations. The most noted of these writers having been bred in the schools of the civil law, imbibed its spirit, and were indebted to it for their fundamental axioms, their definitions, and much of their reasonings.

The doctors of the civil law, ancient and modern, assert the correctness of the doctrine upon the ground of common reason and the evidence of logic. As it is difficult to separate the discussions of the law and the morality, we may as conveniently consider them together. Pothier, while as a judge he allows that the law of his country had wisely considered the interests of commerce and society in refusing to allow traders to get rid of bad bargains, merely because they are bad; yet as a moralist, he maintains that every inequality of price, every sale of a thing for more than it is worth, is void in conscience.

He reasons thus, "Equity ought to preside in all "agreements. Hence it follows, that when one of "the contracting parties gives or does something "for the purpose of receiving any thing else as a "price for it, any injury suffered by him, although, "the other party had used no deceit to cause it, will "alone render that contract vicious. For as equity "in matters of traffic consists in equality, when "equality is violated, or when one of the parties "gives more than he receives, the contract fails "for want of the equity by which it ought to "be governed. Besides, the consent of the injur-"ed party has not in fact been gained, for he would "not have given what he does give, except upon "the false supposition that what he was receiving "in return was of equal value; nor would he have "been disposed to give it at all, if he had known "that what he was to receive was worth much "less."*

Cambaceres the Ex Arch-Chancellor of the French empire, a man who, whatever may have been his political or private character, will leave an enduring name from the important share which he contributed towards the formation of the Civil Code, and the large views and sound learning which he displayed in discussing its grounds and reasons; thus argues in the Council of State: "A fundamen-

* Pother : Traité des Obligations, P. 1. Sec. 33.

" tal article of the Code lays down this definition. " A contract is commutative when one party en- " gages with the other to do or to give something, " which is regarded as the equivalent of that which " he receives. But if there is no contract, except " where one receives the equivalent of what he gives, " how is it possible to refuse to set aside a pretended " contract where one gives all, and the other little " or nothing."*

On this point, the speculative doctrines of Grotius, Wolf, Puffendorf, Rutherforth,† indeed of all the writers of the law of nature and nations cited and referred to by statesmen, lawyers, and moralists,

* Discussions du Code, Tom. II. p. 489.

† There is no writer upon these subjects, snperior to Rutherforth. He is often prolix and diffuse, wasting his words and the students patience in needless discussions of plain propositions. Still he is commonly sound and clear. It is a singular circumstance, that while the books on natural Law and Ethics written by lawyers and statesmen like Grotius and Puffendorf, are overloaded with scholarship and have more allusions to the affairs of antiquity than to any thing that exists in the world as it is in these days ; the writings of two English doctors of divinity, Paley and Rutherforth, are specially remarkable for their original sagacity and adaptation to the conduct of human life. I do not think that on this point, Rutherforth shows his usual accuracy, but I extract his remarks as containing the substance of all that has been said on inadequacy of price by moralists.

" Neither of the parties in a contract can claim any right by virtue of it, " which the other does not consent to transfer to him. And it appears from " the nature of contracts of mutual benefit, that neither of the parties has, or " can be supposed to have, any design or intention of transferring any right to " the other without receiving an equivalent. From hence it follows, that, when " either party has received more than he has given an equivalent for, he has " received what the other never designed or consented should be his : and con- " sequently, as he has no claim to what he has so received, the contract is ei- " ther void or must be corrected, that so he, who has too little, may either have " his own again, or else may have amends made to him.

are little more than elaborate expansions of this argument.

Thus, here is no common accumulation of great authorities. Perhaps, too, it would seem at first sight, that the maxim that it is knavish to sell a thing for more than it is worth, is too self-evident to need the aid of any authority whatever.

"It may indeed be said, when I have bought goods, and have paid the mo- " ney for them, that, by my act of parting with my money and taking the goods, " I planely showed my consent to transfer my property in the money to the " seller, upon condition of his transferring his property in the goods to me.— " But the answer to this is obvious: in buying and selling, it is well known, " from the very nature of the contract, though our words may not express so " much, that neither the buyer nor the seller intend to give each other any " thing, as matter of mere bounty, but only upon supposition of each receiving " an equivalent for what he gives. If therefore I buy goods; I transfer the " property in my money to the seller, upon supposition, that I receive an equi- " valent for what I so transfer, and not otherwise. So that if this supposition " fails, if I do not receive an equivalent, the condition fails, upon which alone " I consented that the money should be his. For this reason, though he may " be in possession of the money, he has no right to it: he can have no right to " it, unless I consented to give him such right; and I never consented to give " him such right, but under the condition jnst now mentioned. In like man- " ner, if I hire a house or lands, that is, if I purchase the use of them; my in- " tention, according to the nature of this contract, is, that I will give the owner " nothing without receiving an equivalent for it. There is nothing of mere " bounty in contracts of this sort; each party designs to receive as much bene- " fit, as he gives. Whatever rent therefore the owner of the house, or land " receives of me, I consent to make it his, upon supposition that I receive the " value of it in the use of his estate. If then this supposition fails, though he " may have gotten possession of my money, it is not his; because it cannot be " his without my consent, and I consented to make it his, only upon supposition " of my receiving an equivalent, which I have not received. The same reason- " ing may be applied to other contracts." Rutherforth's Institutes of Natural Law, B. 1. Chap. 13, Sec. 11.

The student who is desirous to pursue the subject may consult GROTIUS de Jure Belli ac Pacis, Lib. II. cap. 12. HEINECCIUS, Prelectiones, de Cont:— Also, his Elem. Jur. Nat. & WOLFF. Institut. Jur. Nat. et Gent. All of whom agree with Rutherforth.

But it is easy to deceive ourselves with words. To sell a thing for more than it is worth,—simple, as the phrase is, has more than one meaning. It may mean that the seller has taken advantage of his customer's ignorance, and his confidence in the seller's honesty, to charge him three dollars for what he can get any where else for two. This, no doubt, is knavery. But when the great doctors of the civil, and of natural and of public law, say that a sale is unfair, if an equivalent is not given and received; and when they add, that every honest sale proceeds upon the supposition of exchanging equivalents; singular as it may seem, they require what never occurs, or is ever likely to occur, in any commercial transaction. It is not true in any sense, that bargains and sales are made with a view of giving and receiving equal values. All contracts in the way of trade, all purchases of things bought to sell again, are expressly and avowedly made with a view to *profit*. The merchant sells his cotton to his neighbour for cash; with this money he buys copper—and why? Because, to him, in his estimation, cotton is worth less than money, and the copper again is worth more. So, in the pettiest traffic of retail: Every man judges for himself, whether or no the book, the hat, the whip, or the gun, which he is about to buy, is not worth more to him in use or in pleasure, than the money asked for it. If he does not think so, he does not buy. The seller judges in the same way on his side; if he cannot get more than his wares cost him, he will not sell.

In the ordinary routine of business, it commonly happens that both parties decide rightly as to their own interests; but both may be wrong, or either, and the bargain nevertheless an honest one, in the judgment of all men of common sense.

It is self-evident that the notion of giving and receiving mere equivalents, never enters the mind of those who carry on a wholesale trade, or who buy and sell from motives of commercial speculation. This fact alone is sufficient to prove the falsity of a doctrine which, whilst it places morality in obvious contradiction to the necessities and the prosperity of civilized society, is so diametrically opposite to the moral judgments we every hour silently pass on the fairness of men's dealings with each other.

In the common affairs of life, as in our dealings with the baker and the shoemaker, it would seem at the first glance that this doctrine might hold good. This is more in appearance than in reality. The constant competition of the market has fixed a nearly uniform price upon articles of common and domestic use, so that when I buy a pair of shoes, it may seem that the shoemaker and I exchange equal values, because he could sell his shoes at the same price to another customer, and I at the same expense, buy as good shoes at another shop.

But consider a moment. Suppose that instead of buying the shoes of the shoemaker at the current rate, I offer to sell him a pair at the rate he sells his own goods, or even less. If this sale were exchanging equivalents, or any thing like it, he ought to take my shoes as a matter of course. The truth is, that he too, like the merchant, sells what to him is worth less, (and in most traffics of retail, very much less,) for that price which is so far from being an equivalent, that it brings him a profit of fifty or even an hundred per cent.

Moreover, we may ask, how is this imaginary equality to be reconciled with the confessedly fair profits of a monopoly price?—As where a patent protects the rights of an inventor, or peculiarities of soil give to some favoured spot, such as the vineyards of La Fitte, Clos-Vogeot, or Johanisberg, the sole power of supplying any large demand. The wine or the goods, cost a given sum in their production; a sum therefore sufficient to replace the capital and labour expended with the ordinary profits, is the only equivalent that can be assigned. Yet who doubts that it is just and conscientious to get as much for such products or manufactures as the competition of buyers will give? It may be said that the value of the patent or monopoly must be taken into account besides. This seems specious. But let us reflect what that value is. It is nothing else than this very power of selling goods for more than their cost, without being disturbed by other rivals, whose underbidding would bring them down to the market rate. According to the very terms of the proposition, if contracts are void for want of equality, such monopolies, whether the gift of nature, or the result of personal ingenuity, are void in conscience, and ought to be so in law.

The same remarks apply with equal force to any rise of price from scarcity. My flour has cost me, in raising the grain, manufacturing, and bringing it to the place of sale, it may be, four dollars a barrel, including reasonable profits. A foreign demand occurs, flour rises to ten dollars a barrel; four dollars the barrel is the natural equivalent, or else so much of other things as costs four dollars; but where is the immorality of my taking the market price? And how unjust as well as foolishly impolitic, would be the law that prohibited the receiving of it!

It is then wholly incorrect to argue as great lawyers, great divines, and great legislators have done, that when I buy goods, I transfer my property in my money to the seller, upon the supposition that I receive an equivalent for what I transfer, and not otherwise; so that if I do not receive an equivalent, the condition on which I consented to transfer, fails.

On the contrary, if we look into our own minds,

and see what actually passes through our thoughts when we make a bargain, we shall perceive that the true statement of the matter is more nearly this: When I buy, I transfer my money to the seller upon condition of receiving that which I now judge to be in some way or other, more useful, more valualuable, or more agreeable to me than my money. I may judge erroneously in the matter, but certainly the correctness of my judgment as to my own tastes or interests, forms no part of the contract, and cannot affect it.

All this seems to me to be too clear for argument; and were the error confined to pure speculation, it might well be suffered to rest undisturbed, with other venerable errors in the learned volumes of its authors and defenders. But here, false theory has passed from the closet of the philosopher into senates and courts of justice. The reasoning or the authorities of Grotius, Puffendorf, and Pothier, have misled such men as Portalis, and Cambaceres;* have indirectly influenced the opinions of Wedderburn, and Kent, and thus become embodied in codes, or have governed the decisions of learned and upright judges.

The practical inconveniences and absurdities

* The authors or compilers of the French civil code, were Portalis, Tronchet, Bigot-Preameneu, and Moleville. Cambaceres reported a project of a code sometime before, which was a part of the materials used by the commissioners. He also took a very leading part in the discussions in the council of state, where numerous alterations were made.

which are fairly deducible from this doctrine, either as a guide of conscience or a rule of law, offer the best demonstration of its theoretical unsoundness. We have just seen how the experience of modern times, on the continent of Europe, has limited its operation to real estate. The more stationary value of landed property in such countries as France and Flanders, renders the law capable of being applied with more justice and utility there and to that kind of property, than in any other cases. Yet in France during the tempestuous times of the republic, and the days of *assignats*, *mandats territoriaux*, and the other wild inventions of a government paper credit unsupported by pledged capital, or public confidence, it was found impossible to be executed. It must of course be so whenever currency is uncertain, or the title of property insecure, or its value subject to great fluctuations. In France, one man had full confidence in the stability of the republic, another, with more sagacity, or more ardent loyalty, looked forward to the speedy return of the Bourbons and the restoration of confiscated property to its original owners. The estimate, which two such men would put on property, must be widely different, and no one could doubt that a fair and honest bargain might be made between them, although in the unbiassed estimation of judges and arbitrators, the property was sold for less than seven-twelfths of its worth.

In Great Britain, the transition from war to peace, from an over-issued and depreciated paper currency, to one of gold, with the peculiar effect of the corn laws, produced similar results. The price of real estate was for a while nominal. Those whose interest induced them to sell, could not obtain that price, which those who were able and willing to hold their property, considered as its full worth. Many consulted their interest in selling, and so doubtless did most of those who continued to hold. If, whenever a state of doubt and fluctuation of price thus occurs, the civil law rules were applied, men might receive compensation for sales which were in fact far more beneficial to them than keeping their property. In the United States, land is still more an article of commerce, and passes from hand to hand, with the greatest facility. We all know how much its price depends, not only on external circumstances, but on those peculiar to the buyer and seller. The monied man buys western lands or vacant city lots, at what he believes to be less than half their worth. He probably judges rightly: to him they are worth twice their cost. But the seller who could not afford to keep an unproductive property, while he has the means of making an immediate productive application of the money he may receive for it, has also made a good sale, and has no right to complain of inadequacy of price. Every one, who has dealt in lands, or who like myself, has been an observant "looker-on here in Venice," may recall to his memory hundreds of instances to which no rule of law, founded upon the notion of equality of price, could be applied without gross injustice in the particular case, and the worst influence on the general policy of the nation.

From these considerations, and those above stated, I am compelled to say, that I cannot find either in the Roman law, or the jurisprudence of Continental Europe, a perfectly satisfactory and clearly defined law of contracts, so far as it is influenced by inequality of price, or of knowledge.

The doctrines of the civilians bear the impression of a high and pure morality. Yet in theory they are,—I am sensible of seeming presumptuous in saying so,—radically erroneous; and their policy is without question inapplicable to the real state of the multifarious concerns, and varied interests of modern civilized life. To my mind, one of the strongest proofs of this that can be desired, will be found in the fact of the numerous deviations which the civil lawyers have made from their own broad and imposing theory.

It affords a singular commentary upon the whole, that after inculcating the most exalted rules of disinterestedness, the Digest itself preserves the opinion of a great Roman jurist, who qualifies its higher morality, by adding that "the law of nature itself allows men to *cheat a little*, in buying and selling." *In pretio emtionis et venditionis naturaliter licere contrahentibus se circumvenire.*"*

This strange concession to human frailty could only have been made from the necessity of softening the impracticable rigour of the law so as to adapt it to the nature and wants of mankind. It is a strong proof of what, to an observer of human nature, needs no proof, that every attempt to enforce an overstrained and ascetic morality, overshoots its mark, and the ultimate result is a secret laxity of principle, and sometimes an open licentiousness of practice.

* Pomponious in the Digest IV. 4—16—4.

CHAPTER IV.

Occasion of this inquiry—Question what is Price, and how formed—Its variableness—Inadequacy of price—Positive fraud—Concealment in sales—Reservation of what facts equivalent to fraud—What advantages are justifiable and fair.

THE reader who has accompanied me through the rapid sketch, which has been given of the jurisprudence of Europe and our own country, in relation to the ethics and the law of contracts, may, perhaps, think that as the stoical morality is said to have misled the ancient civilians, so I, in my turn, have followed that skeptical philosophy, which loves to assail established opinions, to suggest doubts, and raise difficulties without aiming to discover truth. But it is not so. The purely skeptical spirit is equally dangerous in all moral inquiries; and it was with singular sagacity, that Cicero, long ago, denounced it as peculiarly destructive to sound and sober legal science.

My honest object has been to show the great importance of the subject, the true nature of its difficulties, and the lights which law and theoretical ethics furnish towards its solution. I wished too, to conduct the reader over the same road by which my own mind unexpectedly came to the conclusion, that neither of those venerable legal systems that have so long governed the civilized world, has established, and consistently and uniformly applied, any distinct and clearly defined principles regulating the validity of contracts, so far as they are affected by inequality of price, or by studied or accidental concealment of those circumstances important to the bargain, which are known to one party, and unknown to the other.

This was not with me an inquiry of idle or theoretical curiosity. It grew out of the business of life, as it passed under my own eyes. Some months ago there occurred one of those seasons of wild commercial speculation and unaccountable fluctuations of demand and price, which like epidemics, from time to time without any perceptible cause, visit and afflict the mercantile world. In the course of the negotiations and sales, which then took place of large quantities of those great staple commodities which are most affected by foreign demand, purchases to a vast amount were made, in consequence of private intelligence received and acted upon, before the holders of the goods in question, were, or possibly could be apprized of the rise in price. The case of the New Orleans tobacco, was repeated with every possible variation, and upon the largest scale. Loud complaints of fraud, or at least of unfairness, were made; legal advice was taken, and the whole subject became a common topic of conversation among commercial men. This at length led to newspaper discussion. Different views were taken of the morals of trade; and with regard to the law, though it was generally considered as having been settled by judicial authority, there were not wanting lawyers, who professed and supported the higher principled doctrines of Pothier.

In turning the subject in my own mind, whilst I had little difficulty in deciding on the morality of a single given case, I found it much less easy to lay down any general rules or definitions, at once comprehending all that strict integrity enjoined, and not requiring too much. In applying the rule of private conscience to the regulation of external law, new exceptions and limitations suggested themselves. Thus the necessity of a still higher degree of precision and clearness became more apparent at every step.

With very strong, but ill-defined, impressions of what the doctrine ought to be, I resorted to the examination of our Law, trusting by a comparison not only of analogous decided cases, but of analogous heads of jurisprudence, to be enabled to deduce one broad and harmonious principle, consonant throughout with our natural notions of right and wrong; or, only so far altered and limited in the legal application, as the public good, or, as obvious necessity might imperatively require.

The reader has seen in brief the honest result of this inquiry.

Our law of contracts unquestionably decides numerous particular cases with perfect equity; it lays down many judicious and useful rules for the government of certain sorts of transactions; and wherever its leading cases and original principles have been dictated by such intellects as those of Hardwicke and Mansfield, it is full of light and truth.

But the reasoning and doctrines of these master-minds, cannot always be reconciled with that more ancient part of the law, which bears the stamp of the uncommercial and narrow age in which it originated. Sometimes, too, they are as expressly overruled by the most modern decisions.

Much of this dissonance has naturally passed from the law of England into that of the States of the American Union. The number and independence of the State Tribunals, while they have had a happy effect in liberalizing our law, and preparing the way for future improvement, have yet diminished its present certainty and consistency. The ordinary leaning of our courts has been to the more liberal side, but their course has been neither uniform nor bold. The prudence and learning of our ablest judges have often combined to make them yield to the weight of English authorities, while their judgments openly rejected the reasoning upon which those decisions were avowedly founded.*

The Civil Law, with that of modern continental Europe, and the books of natural and international jurisprudence, seemed to promise a more satisfactory result.

In passing from the domain of Westminster-Hall into the territory of the "Written Law,"† we breathe a new atmosphere, and walk in a clearer light :—

"Largior hic campos æther, et lumine vestit
"Purpureo,——————————."

Here, principles are fixed, definitions settled, and the deductions drawn and applied to particular examples, with an exact and ingenious logic. Setting aside the political and criminal jurisprudence of Rome, I cannot doubt that her Civil Code in most

* It is easy to see in the Reports of the American State Courts, a frequent struggle in the minds of the Court between the respect due to well-settled English precedent, and the obvious inapplicability of the doctrine to the usages and wants of our state of society. Thus in a leading case on the Law of Sales, Seixas *v.* Woods, 2 Caines, 55. Kent, (then a Judge of the N. Y. Supreme Court,) after saying, that "the ancient and uniform language of the English law, made "this a clear case," adds ; "yet, if the question were *res integra* in our law, I "confess, I should be overcome by the reasoning of the civilians;" which is "precisely the reverse of the English Law.

† "*Pays du droit ecrit,*" is the technical name of French jurisprudence for those countries governed by the Roman Law, or by Codes drawn from thence.

of its provisions, deserves all the praises it has received. But on the subject of the present inquiry, I was obliged to think, that its doctrines, admirable in some respects, are in others mixed with error. This arises partly, as has been already stated, from the introduction of a false metaphysic in relation to equality, or the exchange of equivalents in buying and selling; and partly from its having confounded the separate requisitions of justice and benevolence, and thus laid down as the rule of judicial equity, a morality transcending what in the ordinary condition of human life, is always strictly required by private conscience. The modern limitations of this rule, while they prove its defects, go to an opposite extreme. They have doubtless in the hands of wise judges, been sufficient, with some latitude of interpretation, for the administration of a coarse but useful equity. Still they are wholly arbitrary, and depend on no principle.

The whole investigation, though thus unsatisfactory, was very useful. The comparison of the real legislation of different ages and countries, and the examination of cases occurring in actual litigation, are the surest correctives of speculative error. Our dissent from whatever seems irrational or impolitic, marks out, on either side, the limits within which truth must be sought. Thus an ordinary mind may be instructed by the mistakes, as well as by the wisdom, of the wise and great.

With this preparation, let us lay aside the volumes of reporters and civilians, and endeavour without their further help, to deduce for ourselves, from the nature and reason of things, and our own intuitive views of right morals, the safe and sound principles upon which the true equity of contracts must universally rest. Having settled the plain ethics of the question, it will be an after consideration to trace out, how far, or with what modifications, the law of conscience ought also to be that of public justice.

Here, by the way, it will not be superfluous to remind the reader, that the single object of our inquiry is the rule of strict justice, and no more. No little confusion has been suffered to creep into our reasonings on such subjects, by mingling with this, the other and differing considerations of liberality, of benevolence, of personal reputation, or of Christian duty. But, we do not ask what is the course of conduct which his sense of honour would dictate to a liberal and high-spirited man, who blushes to receive the profits of a hard bargain from his poorer neighbour. Nor do we seek what might in many cases, be the conduct of the conscientious Christian, whose religion may sometimes forbid him to enforce his undoubted rights, and make him content to say with the Apostle, "Why do you not rather take wrong? why do you not rather suffer yourselves to be defrauded?" But we ask, what should be the rule of action of such a man as either of these, in those circumstances, where neither duty, nor honour, will allow him to abandon his strict rights: Where, for instance, he cannot yield to the impulse of liberality, without doing injustice to his family or his creditors, or where he acts as the representative of others, as the executor of a friend or the guardian of an orphan, or the business-partner of a commercial house; in fact, in any of those innumerable situations, where no man has a right to go beyond what mere equity prescribes, and where we must all be just before we can have a right to be generous.

The question is, simply, What is the exact measure of that justice which we may claim as a matter of strict right from others—of that justice, which he who violates is not simply hard or avaricious, but absolutely dishonest?

With these objects steadily in view, let us now endeavour to ascertain what are precisely the circumstances which constitute fairness or unfairness in buying and selling. The clue to the accurate solution of this question is, I think, not to be found, where the old lawyers and moralists alone sought it, in metaphysical definitions or logical distinctions. We should rather seek it in some of the plainer truths of political economy.

This is a science of modern growth, and it is curious to note how many of its simplest and most elementary truths escaped the sagacity of the wisest of former days.

I begin then by inquiring, " *What is* PRICE? What are the elements which form it? What, abstracted from all reference to right and wrong are the common considerations which enter into the minds of the buyer and seller in making a bargain?

The acute and profound analysis of Ricardo has resolved all exchangeable value into its original elements of human labour, directly applied or accumulated in capital; and he has clearly traced the few simple, but universal and beautiful laws which govern its operation. But these considerations do not immediately enter into the common reasoning by which men are governed in matters of traffic.

The simplest form of sale or exchange which occurs, (it is of course also the earliest,) is where the parties to the bargain agree upon the terms of the transfer, without considering any other circumstances regulating the value of the things bought and sold, than that comparison which each man makes for himself of his own use for the commodities, or the pleasure he may derive from them, with the price asked, and his own means of payment. Into these considerations the other party does not enter; for, he too, makes a comparison for himself, founded upon views and opinions depending wholly on his own peculiar notions of his interest, upon his inclinations, his taste, and his wealth or poverty. It is evident, that these views and opinions may be widely different on the two sides; so that the terms of the bargain are finally adjusted by some kind of compromise, inclining more or less to one side or the other, according to the stronger necessities, or desires of either party. All that either has a right to claim is, that there should be no lie told, no trick used, to make the subject of the bargain appear, or be thought, to be better, or other than it is in fact.

In a very rude state of society, this is the character of all commerce, without exception; and in the most polished and mercantile communities, it still holds good as to all things which are *unique*, or very peculiar, in their kind, of which there is no regular supply from the soil, or from human labour; and of course no regular market value. Here, then, price depends wholly on the opinions and means of the buyer and seller; and here, consequently, there can be no such thing as inadequacy of price. Whether it be one savage bartering with another his yams and pigs for iron nails, and glass beads, or an affluent English nobleman offering his thousands to his brother peer for a picture of Claude Lorraine, or for the most famous race-horse on the turf; whatever price the means and desires of the buyer will induce him to give, and at which the means and desires of the owner induce him to sell, is the equal price, and the fair price. What other price can there be, than that which those who want a thing, are able and willing to give for it, when it cannot be got elsewhere for less?

This kind of valuation sometimes, also, occurs in a sort of bargaining which is indicative of the most advanced and artificial state of society. It is the buying and selling of speculation, where purchases are made of lands peculiarly situated, or goods are bought, not with reference to present use or profit, but with relation to a future, and anticipated state of the market.

A man of large capital in passing through some hamlet in a newly settled country, is impressed with the conviction that from local advantages this now neglected spot is destined to become the centre of commerce to a large and wealthy district. Relying upon this judgment, he determines to buy the property. As land, it is worth almost nothing, and there may be no other bidders for it. But the sagacious proprietor has the same views or opinions with him who wishes to buy. The reasoning of each man, as to the greater or less profits which he might derive from a certain sum of money, compared with the profits of the lands; their ideas of the future value of the property itself; all this is private, and personal to each. Neither thinks of communicating such views to the other. In the comparison of mutual offers, the property may be finally disposed of at a price which, to all others than the parties, may seem wild and absurd. Yet each has received, not, to be sure, an equivalent, but, what he himself judges to be, to him, worth more than what he parts with. In such bargains between intelligent and sagacious men, the experience of our own country has a thousand times shown, that it commonly turns out that both were right. If either be a loser, he can only say, that he erred in his calculations.

But, in the ordinary concerns of civilized life, in buying and selling articles of domestic use or consumption, or in the wholesale operations of trade in the great staple productions of a country's agriculture or manufactures, some new elements in the formation of price, make their appearance, entering openly or secretly into all our calculations.

All objects largely in demand, and of a supply at all proportioned to it, of constant consumption and regular production, or, on any account whatever, of frequent bargain and sale, are soon brought by the competition of the market, and the operation of supply and demand, and cost of production, to some general averages of price, fluctuating from time to time, according to the operation of various causes, but always closely and certainly depending upon a few general facts, (the result of numerous smaller particulars,) relating to demand, cost, or quality. Thus arises that Market Price which every buyer or seller must take into calculation, or else without calculating, consent to be governed by.

An ordinary bargain, then, does not result from the individual and secret wishes, opinions, and judgments, of the parties alone; but in addition to these, a common set of facts must also enter into the calculations of both sides.

You are negotiating for the purchase of a ship. Your knowledge and experience in shipping, may give you a great superiority over me and others, in the selection of a sound and fast sailing vessel: you may have, too, some very special purpose for a brig of a certain burden, of a given draft of water, or kind of equipment,—all which would induce you to pay more for such a vessel than any other person. These are considerations for your own direction. On the other hand, the ship-owner has, also, his private considerations. He may be tired of the business, may be anxious to wind up his concerns; or, has pressing calls for money. But, beside these inducements to sell, or buy, both of you take into calculation some common facts, upon which you mutually reason. You both ask, how do ships now sell in this port? What is the cost of building such a brig as this? &c. &c.

In important and very deliberate negotiations, the whole of this process of reasoning is distinctly developed. In the every-day matters of retail, there is so little inducement to chaffer, the business is so much an affair of routine, and the considerations peculiar to either party, are so few, that when wewant a loaf of bread, or a quire of paper, we pay the price asked ; taking it for granted, that the seller's honesty, or prudence, will prevent him from demanding more than it can be bought for elsewhere.

Thus, wherever there is a market value, there are some facts which both parties to a bargain either actually take into calculation, or else the one relies upon the other's honesty to do so for both. The concerns of trade are so multifarious that it is not easy to define, in terms admitting of no exception, what those facts are. They may, however, be broadly summed up as *those facts which necessarily, directly and materially, influence the estimate on which the market value is founded, and therefore enter, of course, into the calculations of all dealers of ordinary prudence, and acquaintance with the business.*

Besides external circumstances affecting computations of price, such as cost, scarcity, or foreign demand, there must be included among these facts, as necessarily entering into all calculations, some estimate of the quality of the particular thing bought and sold. Individuals differ widely in their tastes, in the uses to which they mean to apply the same thing, in the judgment and estimates they frame of the worth of any given commodity. Hence, the worth of any given commodity. Hence, in respect to the goodness and quality of an article offered for sale, the buyer and seller, to a certain extent, may each have his private views which concern himself only. But the average market price always supposes the article to have the common and ordinary qualities which cause the usual demand for things of that kind. Whether or not the subject of the bargain is fit for the ordinary purposes to which such things are applied? whether it possess the properties which give the current value to similar commodities?—These are leading questions which must enter into the estimate that any man of ordinary intelligence would form of their worth, in exchange or sale. If the flour is sour; if the beef is tainted; if the horse sold is unsound—the several articles, whatever value they may retain for other uses, have no longer the properties which make them useful, or desirable, to the great mass of those whose demand fixes their current price.

In this manner we see that, as in all things not the objects of regular supply and demand, price is the result only of the *individual* views and opinions of the parties; in those things which are so, it is the result of such views and opinions on each side, taken in conjunction with the *common* considerations of quality, market price, and whatever else would enter into the estimate of any other intelligent persons under the same external circumstances. These individual considerations may sometimes vary price immensely from its ordinary rate. Then, again, their influence is so slight as scarcely to affect it.

Nothing can be more variable than price, in which ever of these ways it is settled. The market rate of all goods is constantly changing. A slight scarcity of any thing in common use, and which cannot be instantly produced in any quantity to meet the demand, such as wheat, or wool—amounting, it may be, but to a falling off of one-tenth of the quantity usually furnished,—will frequently double the price. Or, the quantity continuing the same, the opening of a new market will, in the same way, double or treble the worth of the whole. A speculative demand in anticipation of a supposed future scarcity, often produces yet greater fluctuations. Cotton is to-day sold at ten cents the pound: in a few weeks it rises to fifty; and in another month is to be had at its first cost. The market price, thus irregular as it is, may again be greatly varied by the individual judgments and means of buyers and sellers. There is, then, it is evident, nothing like a permanent value of one commodity, or kind of property, as compared with another.

Still greater is the difference which may be made as to things not subject to the common estimation of the market, by the speculation, the tastes, wants, or caprices of purchasers.

Can there then be any such thing in the literal sense of the words, as adequacy of price, equality or inequality of compensation? In other words; from the very nature of the thing, price depends solely upon the agreement of the parties, being created by it alone. Mere inequality of price, or rather what appears so in the judgment of a third person, cannot, without reference to something else, be any objection to the validity of a sale, or of an agreement to sell.

If a peer chooses to give two thousand guineas for an old story book, for which not one man in a million would give a shilling; if a pastry-cook agrees to give twice as much for a shop of twenty feet square, in a certain street of London or New-York; who is to say that these men are not the best judges of their own interests and pleasures? who has a right to decide whether the purchase is equal or not? who is entitled to pronounce the bargain to be hard or unconscionable simply because he knows of no one else who would give half as much?

Such sales have actually occurred, to the wonder of many; yet the nobleman, who indulged his taste for scarce books at this expense, was not cheated; while the pastry-cook proves by his purchase, not his folly, but his sagacity and enterprise.

Yet if a merchant were to pay me eight dollars a barrel for a cargo of flour which he could have bought of any one else for four, and this in a mere business transaction, without any idea of generosity in the affair, and with nothing special as to the quality of the flour, or in external circumstances; no one would hesitate to say that here is an unequal bargain; all agree that it is one not binding in conscience, and that if the law will afford relief, the loser ought to seek its aid. This is true; but why? Not certainly from the inadequacy of the price, compared with the worth of the flour. This flour was worth that money six months ago, and may be so again six months hence, and would be so at this moment, perhaps, at a few hundred miles distance. It is simply for this reason; since, under such circumstances, no man would pay eight dollars for what he could buy at four, this price proves that the buyer must have been in some way or other misled as to the market price of flour, or the quality of that particular cargo, or some other fact important to fixing its value.

Thus it is that inadequacy in price may afford strong presumptive evidence to an arbitrator or a judge, of some error or fraud in the substance of the contract.

Rebut that presumption, show that all the facts were known, or point out the real motive for giving this extra price; no good reason then remains why the price agreed upon should not be allowed to be an adequate price.

We have now advanced to another stage of the inquiry. What is it that constitutes fraud, or error, so as to affect a contract in natural justice and morality?

This is the purely ethical part of the question, and we have the advantage of approaching it with a more distinct preliminary view of the true state of those facts from which the moral obligation is to be deduced, than has commonly been taken by legal elementary writers and speculative moralists.

It is a self-evident principle apparent to the common sense of all men, and recognised as fundamental by every system of law, not excepting the rudest and most impolitic, that positive fraud invalidates any contract. Fraud, here, is understood to include, not only absolute falsehood, but every trick, artifice, or manœuvre, calculated to excite false expectations, or to mislead one party for the benefit of the other.

No matter whether it be a trick to conceal the intrinsic defects of a piece of goods on sale; or to mislead the buyer as to the extrinsic circumstances which give it its current value, or to influence his private opinions and inclinations by an indirect manœuvre; it alike authorizes the party deceived to consider himself freed from all the obligations of the contract; provided, the fraud has been such, that without that artifice, the agreement either would not have been made at all, or not made upon these terms.

But this Fraud, concerning which all laws, and all moralists agree, must be something positive. The next question is,—how far, and when, may a man, consistently with honesty, keep his superior knowledge to his own breast, and profit by mere silence, from the ignorance of others?

One of the most obvious answers to this question must be, that no man can ever honestly profit by his superior knowledge, whenever there is a confidence expressly or impliedly reposed in him that he will take no such advantage of it, and wherever, too, this confidence is the efficient cause of his being able to take such advantage. If a trustee, or an executor, or a guardian,—if the agent of a merchant, or the steward or attorney of a landholder, is enabled by the knowledge gained from situation, to make a profitable purchase or sale on his own account out of the property confided to him; here legal equity and common moral reason agree in branding the transaction as fraudulent, and declaring the bargain not binding.

This is so, because, it must have been presumed as a condition precedent to the whole business that such superiority of knowledge would never be used against the employer or trustor*: Had it not been for this presumption, the means of gaining such an advantage would never have been given.

* This is an unusual and uncouth word, but I use it, because our language wants a popular substitute to the legal barbarism of *cestui que truste*.

Enlarge this plain principle ; extend and apply it to all contracts of sale: This will I think solve most of the theoretical difficulties that embarrass the inquiry.

For precisely the same reasons that we brand the guilt of the faithless trustee, or dishonest agent, it is just as clear that we may also say in broader terms, that, *It is always fraudulent in contracts, to take advantage in any respect whatever, wherein it is of course presumed by the one side, and understood by the other to be so presumed, that no advantage will be taken.*

This needs no argument to show its moral obligations. For practical purposes the next step is to inquire—

What is the mutual understanding with which men enter into bargains ? What is that difference of knowledge, respecting which it is presumed that no advantage will be taken ? What is that difference which is more or less expected to exist, and which both parties impliedly consent that each other should use ?

My knowledge of my own interests, and my personal necessities, my sagacity, natural or acquired, in forming judgments of the state of the market ; in brief, all that has been above summed up as constituting the facts and reasoning of a bargain, peculiar to each *individual*, can never be expected by the other party to be communicated ; and in most instances it would be impracticable or silly to do so. All know what a wide difference exists among men in these points, and whatever advantage may result from that inequality, is silently conceded in the very fact of making a bargain. It is a superiority on one side—an inferiority on the other, perhaps very great, but they are allowed. This must be so; the business of life could not go on were it otherwise.

Not so with regard to the *common* facts, which immediately and materially affect price in the estimate of the generality of those who buy and sell. It is true, that strict equality of knowledge, as to these points, is just as difficult as with regard to other matters. But the contract is entered into on the supposition, that whatever superiority of knowledge one may have over the other, *no advantage will be taken of it.* This forms the fundamental consideration of the contract.

My hatter unquestionably well understands the worth and cost of his hats, and I know nothing about the matter. But I buy of him on the implied understanding that he will take no advantage of my ignorance, and will charge me what other customers pay. If in consequence of my ignorance, he makes me pay ten dollars for a hat, which those who are better judges get for five, he cheats me.

The merchant whose enterprise discovers a new market for his country's productions, or the chymist, to whom science reveals a new and useful secret of nature, may conscientiously use these advantages in a purchase, because the seller cannot but take it for granted, that such advantage, if possessed, would be used; and because an offer of the current market price, does not involve any intimation that such new use or application may not be contemplated. Not so the flour dealer, who, upon a sudden rise at New-York or Baltimore, buys flour in some district where its price is solely regulated by the demand at those ports, but where the rise is not yet known. This man makes an unfair bargain; because the very act of offering and buying at old prices is a practical assertion, relied on by the seller, that the old price is, so far as the buyer knows, still the market price.

Again, take a stock transaction.

I am a director and large stockholder of an Insurance Company. From my observation and experience in the concerns of the institution, I form an opinion that the business of insurance is overdone, and that the present rates of premium are not an average compensation for the whole risks assumed; so that the profits of any particular company must depend on mere good fortune. With these impressions, I sell out my insurance stock to vest my funds elsewhere. Perhaps he who buys my stock, has far less knowledge of this subject, than I have. But the facts on which I form my judgment are accessible to many, and others may deduce a very different inference from them. The buyer knows that there is a great difference among men in their management of their money concerns, and their knowledge of all that relates to it, and this, he has no reason to suppose may not also exist between him and me. Unless there is some special confidence between us, other than that arising from the mere sale, he has no right to presume that I will not use this difference to my best advantage ; just as he will on his own side.

But, if I had intelligence of distant losses, which have sunk half of our capital, and I and my brother directors conceal it until we have disposed of our own stock at the current rate, this is no longer a fair use of superior knowledge. Here the sale of stock, at what was its market rate before an event which must so materially and necessarily lessen its value, is an indirect assertion on my part that I know of no such event; while the purchase is made in consequence of the buyer's not knowing of such a loss himself, and his confidence in me, that I have no such secret knowledge.

These two cases of the stock-dealer are extreme and marked cases. Between them, there are many shades which gradually soften into each other, and cannot well be described in any general rule. But refer them to the leading principle of the degree of confidence reposed and taken advantage of, and there is little difficulty in their solution.

Our two New-Orleans merchants met to buy and sell a cargo of tobacco. The seller may well presume that the inferences and probabilities relating to the prospect of peace and the demand for tobacco, might be quite different in the buyer's mind, from what they were in his own. If one party choose to communicate his private reasons for making a given offer, it is well; if he does not do so, the other could not claim it, and the bargain goes on as before.

But if the owner had suspected that an advantage was to be gained over him from his ignorance of some fact of such a nature as to alter materially the common estimate of price among all who buy or sell tobacco in that market, he would never have entered into the negotiation until he was better informed concerning it. The very making a bargain, with reference to a supposed state of affairs on which the market price depended, is an indirect assertion made on the one side, and an implied confidence reposed on the other, as to the actual existence of a certain state of affairs.

Every person who bought or sold at New-Orleans, looked upon the war and blockade, as a material cause of the low prices. These were facts, common to all calculations. Opinions of *individuals* differed as to the chance of their duration, and a greater or less sagacity in such opinions, was an understood and allowed advantage in all the trade carried on there. But the knowledge of the actual fact of peace, and the concealment of it, amount to the seizing an advantage, where the contract itself was formed upon the understanding that no such advantage would be taken.

The concealment was therefore dishonest and fraudulent; consequently, the bargain, if the seller objected to its execution, void in conscience.

Let us next place our tobacco dealers in another point of view. They both know very well that, among those who buy or sell tobacco, there may be some better and some worse judges than themselves of the article, as to those particular qualities which give it a preference in certain markets, or fit it for particular manufactures. Of this special and peculiar skill, each fairly takes his chance, and neither has any right to complain, if he finds that he has not made as good a sale or purchase as he might have done. But if the seller (without using any art) knows that these hogsheads of tobacco, which appear to be of a particular growth, are in fact filled up with refuse leaves, or with tobacco of a less valuable kind, and suffers the buyer to mislead himself, is silent as to defects, and sells at the current price of the choicest tobacco, who doubts that this is fraud? Why is it so? Because, a certain average of quality is one of those common facts which enter into the estimate of all dealers, and the sale at a given price, is evidence enough of a presumption in the mind of the buyer, that the tobacco was of the quality commonly sold at that rate; and because the advantage of possible superior information on such a fact, was so far from being allowed by him, that the mere suspicion of it would have put an end to the purchase.

Yet if either party gives notice that in any particular instance he is to be answerable for no faults or defects; or if by selling at auction, or in any other way that the usages of trade point out, he tacitly makes this understood; this confidence is at an end. The seller gives notice, that it does not comport with his interests or convenience to receive the confidence which would otherwise be reposed upon him. It is then no longer reposed. The buyer has no right to presume any thing, and must judge for himself; no matter how much the price differs from what others pay, no one under these circumstances can complain of unfairness. This exception decisively points out what the principle is.

From these views we may deduce a broader rule as to concealment or reservation, which may be laid down as that of strict natural justice. It may be thus expressed.

Whenever any advantvge is taken in a purchase, or sale, from the suppression of any fact, (not of an opinion or inference,) *necessarily and materially affecting the common estimate which fixes the present market value of the thing sold; and in regard whereto, the sale alone conclusively proves, that it was presumed by the losing party, that no advantage would be taken; such advantage is gained by* FRAUD.

This rule embraces most of our ordinary business transactions. But there is a class of cases of no unfrequent occurrence, where the reference to the market value is less direct. This occurs when both parties understand that the motive of the purchase is some special use, or purpose, understood on both sides. Here the same principle will still govern, but it must be applied with a slight modification.

I am bargaining for a horse. My avowed object is, to get a gentle and easy saddle horse, for an invalid. The horse's age, beauty, or speed, are matters of comparative indifference to me. The owner is told of all this. It then becomes unfair for him to conceal from me any fact which, if known, would convince me that the horse would not answer my end, though it might not be considered as the slightest objection, or fault, by any other person. By agreeing to take the horse, without special warranty, I repose my confidence in the owner that no advantage will be taken of me in that respect. On many other points we repose no special confidence in each other. Our skill in horse flesh, our knowledge of the horse-market, of what our private affairs, or convenience, will enable us to give, or refuse, are our own, and we may make the most of them.

Here, then, the former rule would require to be modified somewhat in this way:

In every contract where some special use or purpose is understood between the parties to be the inducement of the bargain, it is unjust to take advantage from the suppression of any fact, relating to the object of the contract, such as if known would affect the value of the object in the estimation of any reasonable person, having the same intention as to its use; however he might differ from the actual party in information, or in external circumstances.

On the other hand, it may be confidently and decisively stated, that,

There is nothing dishonest, or unfair, either in using superior sagacity as to probabilities, or in applying greater skill and better knowledge, as to those facts which do not necessarily enter into the common calculations of those who fix the current price, and concerning which no confidence, express or implied, is reposed.

These few rules seem to me to be, in general words, the fair expression of those particular limitations, as to the *suppressio veri*, concealment, and reservation, which common sense and common honesty prescribe. On the one hand, these are far from the hard common law rules, which oblige each party to stand by his bargain, at all risks; and on the other, just as far from the apparently more liberal, but, in truth, extravagant doctrine of Pothier, and the civilians.

The rule of the latter, that the vendor ought to disclose every circumstance within his knowledge, which the vendee has an interest in knowing, and that he who is silent on such circumstances, sins against good faith; when it is applied to particular cases, will often be just. But it will also extend to thousands of other cases, where justice and the good faith of mutual dealings never called for such disclosure, and where, if it were made, it would destroy that fair superiority which the industrious or the bold trader has earned by his labour or enterprise, over the careless and the idly ignorant.

Adopt the common law doctrine as the moral rule, and all men must be taught to regard their neighbours as sharpers, and to deal with them at arms' length. Take the theory of the civil law, and all men of business are put upon the same level as to the uses of skill and information; while the most efficient motives for exertion in the gaining of information in trade, or the useful arts, are denounced as dishonest and unjustifiable.

I have no desire to swell these pages with comments upon the false or imperfect statements of this question to be found in the writers on ethics, and natural law. None of them whose works I have looked into, come so near the truth as Paley, and his remarks on many collateral points are shrewd and just.

But the moral rule which he proposes for the construction of all contracts, and which he thinks capable of being universally applied with great ease and certainty, is certainly inaccurate. He says that:

"Whatever is expected by one side, and known to be so expected by the other, is to be deemed a part, or condition, of the contract."*

The too great latitude of this rule, and the difference between it, and those above proposed, may be best shown, by applying it to a special case or two, selected from among those which the law reports furnish so abundantly.

A village on the banks of one of the great rivers of the United States, had often been spoken of by public men, as a proper site for a national navy-yard. An owner of land there, under the belief that the navy-yard will soon be established at that place, sets a high value on his farm. A wealthier neighbour is of the same opinion, and finally agrees

* Paley. Moral Philosophy, b. iii. c. 6.

to buy his property at twice the price which it is worth, if used for agriculture, or sold for village lots. The dealings are all frank and honest. The buyer and seller each expects, and knows that the other expects, a great increase of value from the future navy-yard. Both are disappointed; the navy-yard is fixed elsewhere, and the property falls to its former value. Here, certainly, Paley's rule fails. There can be no moral obligation here on the seller to make good the deficiency up to the value which the buyer expected, and the seller knew he expected. All that can be said, is, that this was a speculation which turned out unfortunately.

Take another case, under a different aspect.

In one of the feverish excitements of the stock market, a rapid rise in the stock of a particular chartered company takes place; an idea prevails that immense profits will be divided, and that the stock will be in great demand at London or Amsterdam. A cooler headed stockholder, (without being in possession of any special facts inaccessible to others,) believes not a word of all this, and sells out at the current value. The purchaser buys under the confident expectation of a farther rise, and the seller knows this expectation. Yet certainly this result of greater prudence and cooler calculation, ought not to charge the seller in law or in conscience, with the obligation of making good the unfounded speculations of others.

It is evident that Paley has been led to overstate the moral obligation of a contract, from not accurately distinguishing between individual knowledge, those reasonings and expectations concerning which no confidence passes between the parties, and those considerations common to both, respecting which it is stipulated or implied that no advantage shall be taken.

Yet it is due to the respect I cherish for the memory of this excellent and most useful writer to add, that I believe he had the right view of the subject in his mind, though imperfectly developed, and that he needed nothing but the application of a few commercial cares or litigated questions to his doctrines, to have suggested to him all the corrections and limitations which it requires.

CHAPTER V.

Subject continued—Rules and Principles of the preceding chapter recapitulated, and extended to all Contracts of mutual benefit—Contracts of hazard—Cases of mutual error—Implied warranty of sort and quality—Different effects of error, and of intentional concealment.

In the argument of the preceding chapter, no attempt has been made at discovery, or originality. It would be absurd to do so, on a subject with which every body is practically familiar. All that has been aimed at is, to present a distinct and detailed analysis of the thoughts which pass rapidly through the mind in buying and selling, and have become so habitual that we act from the general impression and result of them, without attending to the steps of our own reasoning. If this statement has been correctly made, the attentive reader will recognise in it the processes of his own mind in fixing the price of whatever he has bargained about, and the principles of the moral judgments which he has frequently formed upon his own conduct, or that of others.

It may, at the first view, have seemed paradoxical to assert, that there is no such thing as inadequacy, or inequality, of price. Yet in one, and that a most important sense, necessary to all sound reasoning on the subject, this is certainly true. It is clear that there is no fixed or unchangeable comparative value between one piece of property and another; all depends on the wants and opinions of men, and the ease or difficulty of procuring each several thing. In one state of things, an acre of prime land may be worth as much as a sheep, and either of them may be purchased for a dollar. In another state of the market, the sheep may be worth five dollars, while the same acre is universally estimated as a fair equivalent for twenty sheep. This is by no means an extreme case. Thus every price, understandingly and fairly agreed to, is a fair price.

But there is another sense of inadequacy of price. A price much greater or less than similar things could be bought or sold for at the time, will often afford good evidence of fraud or mistake; since it is not probable that such a bargain could otherwise have been made by any man in his sober senses.

The universal moral judgments of men, intuitively pronounce that in any bargain, he who takes advantage of his neighbour, in any respect where his neighbour confides in him that he will take no such advantage, and where he knows that without that confidence no bargain could have been made, is guilty of fraud, or, at any rate, of unfairness closely approaching to fraud. If this reliance be formally reposed in his integrity by constituting him an agent or guardian of another's rights, here, from the more marked and definite character of that trust, if he misuses it to the injury of him who reposes it, his fraud is of a deep character of guilt. But if his neighbour, without formally so declaring, repose the same sort of confidence in him, by taking it for granted, that he will sell at the market price; that the goods which he offers at the price of good commodities, are, as far as he knows, of a merchantable quality, or of any given kind; it is, for the very same reason, unfair to take advantage of such confidence.

The lottery dealer who, without using any direct falsehood, or artifice, buys or sells, at the price of undrawn tickets, tickets which he knows to be prizes, or blanks, is guilty of a dishonesty which entitles the other party to claim back whatever he has lost by his bargain. Why? Because, the buyer of the blank, or the seller of the prize, in dealing with him as if the ticket were undrawn, must take it for granted, that they are in mutual ignorance of the fate of the ticket, or mutually suppose it to be undrawn; and thus confides in him with whom he bargains, that there is no superiority of knowledge on the matter. The using such a confidence to one's own gain, and the injury of the other party, is the essence of the fraud.

Common sense tells us that there are some peculiar advantages of skill, shrewdness, and experience, regarding which no one ever reposes any confidence that they will not be used, and which without some express stipulations, no one has a right to call upon us to abandon. Here, justice permits us to use our superiority freely. If circumstances allow us to relinquish it, whether we should do so or not, is an affair of generosity, of pride of character, of benevolence, but never can enter into the consideration of strict right.

In order to state the argument without confusion, I have in the preceding chapter, mainly confined the direct consideration of the subject to the Contract of Bargain and Sale. But the principles are of the broadest application, and embrace all commutative contracts.

Under this name of commutative contracts, may be included every case:

Where one party undertakes to do, or to give, any thing which is considered by both parties as a compensation for what is done, or given, or promised to be done or given, by the other.

The morality of every such bargain, whatever may be the subject of it, is governed by the same broad and invariable rules of good faith and sincerity.

It may be a sale of property for money; or an exchange of property for property; or the giving money for personal services; or it may be a contract of hazard, where money is given for the chance of gain, depending upon the occurrence of an uncertain event, as in the purchase of a lottery ticket; or where one chance of gain, depending on an uncertain event, is pledged against another chance, as in wagers, or bets.

In each and all of these contracts, it will be found, on attentive examination, that while some individual considerations may, and frequently must, enter into the bargain, on either side, which the other has no claim to know, and each is justified in using, for his own profit; there are other common facts, without knowing which it would be impossible for any third person to make a reasonable calculation as to the matter, and where, if inferior in actual knowledge, each impliedly reposes full confidence, that such ignorance will not be used by the other to his detriment.

The slightest reflection is sufficient to show that there is not, and there cannot be any valid reason why the same rules of justice which ought to govern the sale of a house or a ship, ought not also to prevail, where the subject of the contract is not the absolute property, but the use of the one and the freight of the other. Nowhere is the truth of these principles more prominently visible than in Contracts of Hazard. Under this somewhat odious name, are conveniently comprehended not only games of chance, and wagers, and lotteries.

but as they are to be calculated on much the same principles, the ingenious financial inventions of Tontines and annuities, and all the various and valuable forms of mercantile insurance.

The nature and degree of fair dealing and equality, required in such transactions, are in practice perfectly well understood. In our own case, self-interest may make us wilfully blind, but few disinterested people will differ in their decisions. In theory, and sometimes in law, their true equity has been mistaken, or misrepresented. They cannot be better stated than it has been done by Paley, whose remarks I quote, because they correspond precisely with the principles above laid down; though they cannot be so exactly reconciled with some of his own previous rules, and definitions:

"What some say of this kind of contracts, that "'one side ought not to have any advantage over "the other,' is neither practicable nor true. It is "not practicable; for that perfect equality of skill "and judgment, which this rule requires, is seldom "to be met with. I might not have it in my pow-"er to play with fairness a game at cards, billiards, "or tennis; lay a wager at a horse-race; or under-"write a policy of insurance, once in a twelve-"month, if I must wait till I meet with a person, "whose art, skill, and judgment, in these matters,

" is neither greater nor less than my own. Nor is " this equality requisite to the justice of the con- " tract. One party may give to the other the " whole of the stake, if he please, and the other " party may justly accept it, if it be given him; " much more, therefore, may one give to the other " a part of the stake; or, what is exactly the same " thing, an advantage in the chance of winning the " whole.

" The proper restriction is, that neither side " have an advantage, by means of which the other " is not aware: for this is an advantage taken, " without being *given*. Although the event be still " an uncertainty, your advantage in the chance has " a certain value; and so much of the stake, as that " value amounts to, is taken from your adversary " without his knowledge, and therefore without his " consent. If I sit down to a game at whist, and " have an advantage over the adversary, by means " of a better memory, closer attention, or superior " knowledge of the rules and chances of the game, " the advantage is fair; because it is obtained by " means of which the adversary is aware; for he is " aware, when he sits down with me, that I shall " exert the skill that I possess, to the utmost. But " if I gain an advantage by packing the cards, " glancing my eye into the adversary's hands, or " by concerted signals with my partner, it is a dis-

"honest advantage; because it depends upon "means, which the adversary never suspects that "I make use of.

"The same distinction holds of all contracts, in-"to which chance enters. If I lay a wager at a "horse-race, founded upon the conjecture I form "from the appearance, and character, and breed "of the horse, I am justly entitled to any advan-"tage which my judgment gives me; but, if I car-"ry on a clandestine correspondence with the "jockies, and find out from them, that a trial has "been actually made, or that it is settled before-"hand which horse shall win the race; all such in-"formation is so much fraud, because derived "from sources which the other did not suspect, "when he proposed or accepted the wager.

"In speculations in trade, or in the stocks, if I "exercise my judgment upon the general aspect "and posture of public affairs, and deal with a per-"son who conducts himself by the same sort of "judgment; the contract has all the equality in it "which is necessary; but if I have access to se-"crets of state at home, or private advice of some "decisive measure or event abroad, I cannot avail "myself of these advantages with justice, because "they are excluded by the contract, which proceed-"ed upon the supposition, that I had no such ad-"vantage."

* Paley's Moral Philosophy: B. iii. part i. c. 8, on Contracts of Hazard.

These observations might have been more fully elucidated by reference to the morality of Marine Insurance. The calculation of the chances of loss, and of the value of insuring against any risk, allows considerable difference between the insurer and the insured, in the degrees of skill and knowledge, as to navigation, or judgment of vessels, of the character of captain and owners, or the state of foreign affairs. The underwriter and the shipowner, each uses, and has a right to use, fairly and without the slightest scruple, any such superiority he possesses, or believes himself to possess. These differences often afford considerable latitude in settling the amount of premium, particularly where there is any thing peculiar, and out of the common track of business, in the voyage and cargo, or the political aspect of foreign affairs.

But if the goods insured are lost, or, at the date of the latest advices, in great danger of being so, and the owner knows it; or, what more rarely occurs, if they are out of danger, and the underwriter knows it, here is a violation of good faith which none can hesitate to pronounce fraudulent.

So far as fraud or unfair reservation affects moral obligation, I can perceive no distinction founded in common sense, between *executed* contracts, that is to say, those already carried into effect, and *executory* ones, which are hereafter to be completed. In both cases the injured party is exposed to loss, by the unfairness of the other. If the bargain remains to be executed, this unfairness releases the injured person from the obligation of performing his stipulations. If it is wholly or in part performed, the sufferer has a just claim that the bargain should be rescinded, and that he should be restored, as nearly as may be, to his former situation. In both cases, since he suffers by the artifice of the other, he is entitled in conscience to be relieved from all the effects of that artifice, and of course to full satisfaction for any indirect or consequential damages he may have thus received. This claim, whatever the courts of law may decide concerning it, the offended party, whenever he comes to a better mind, will find himself in conscience bound to allow.

Another question now presents itself. In a purchase or sale, one party gains, and the other is a serious loser in consequence of the common mistake of both as to some essential fact, of which the intentional concealment by either would have been dishonest. How does this affect the contract?

For example: Suppose that the sale of tobacco at New-Orleans, so often alluded to, had been made at war prices, but under mutual ignorance of the fact of peace. Is such a bargain void? I can see no ground for thinking that it is. It has already been shown that the idea of equivalents in a bargain is visionary. Both parties mean to get what is worth more to them than what they give, and the comparative value of lands, and goods, and money, has no fixed standard.

The contract, so far as regards the main facts on which it was regulated, rests on the presumption, only, of the good faith of the parties in the use of their respective information, not on that of the infallibility of their knowledge. The idea of something occurring to raise the value of the article is one of the inducements to the bargain on the buyer's part, and if his conjecture is immediately realized, this is indeed an advantage gained, but one, the chance of which was impliedly allowed by the other. Thus, if there were no suppression of any fact known to one, that could have influenced the other, there seems nothing wanting that is essential to the validity of the contract.

But wherever the mutual error relates to something intrinsic in the subject of sale, as to the quality, or the nature of the thing sold, there is another view to be taken of it. The bargain is still fair; but how is the execution of it affected by this error?

I buy, or agree to buy, at the highest price, of some one who has as little opportunity of knowing the true character of the goods as myself, a parcel of Shawls. These are represented, and we both believe them to be the beautiful and highly valued Cashmere Shawls of the East. On delivery, they prove to be an inferior imitation of them, manufactured from commoner materials in France or England, not known in trade under the same name, and not of a fourth of the value either for use or for sale.

A brewer buys a cargo of wheat for the avowed purpose of using it in his trade. He pays the usual price for good wheat fit for his purpose, and so the seller supposes it to be. It turns out to be heated, and unfit for malting.

Without any special agreement or description, a merchant buys some bales of cotton, for which he pays the current price of merchantable cotton of that growth and quality. The inside of the bales are filled with refuse cotton of no value.

In neither of these cases is there any formal warranty, nor can any suspicion be entertained that the immediate seller knew of the defect or error, by which he, himself, is perhaps a sufferer.

Here then we have examples of three different classes of mutual mistake. In the first instance, the thing delivered is different in kind from the description given and believed of the thing sold. In the second it differs materially from the peculiar quality expressed and understood between the buyer and seller. In the last, the difference consists in the inferiority to that average degree of goodness which is considered in settling the market price, and which is silently taken for granted to exist wherever the average market price is paid.

In each of these cases, the civil law, as we have seen, and all its derivative systems compel the seller to make good the bargain according to the understanding of it. In each of these, the common law says to the buyer, (in the first case with some hesitation and variance; in the others, without any,)—"You have neglected to obtain an express warranty from the seller, and have therefore taken the risk upon yourself." The judges and teachers of that law, not content with appealing to authority, vindicate, boldly, both the wisdom and justice of this rule.

Setting aside all consideration of the legal policy, the morality and common sense of the matter are not hard to be ascertained. The bargain is simply this:—"Both of us believe that you have a number of Cashmere shawls; under this belief I agree to take of you so many at such a price." Or thus: "I will take of you, at such a price, so much merchantable Sea Island cotton, which we both suppose to be contained in certain bales, in your possession." The bargain is honest and valid. But the supposition fails on which it was made. This is an unlucky mistake for both of us, for the bargain can no longer be executed. The delivery of another thing, widely differing in sort or quality from what we bargained about, is certainly no fulfilment of the agreement. This would be substituting another bargain for that which was actually made. It is making the buyer, instead of offering to give such a price for so much cotton, offer to give the price for so many bales and all that they contain.

This would be reasonable only in those cases, where, by the known usage of trade, or by express agreement, the buyer is understood to take all risks, and to buy, not a certain quantity of merchandise, but a particular parcel, or box, or bale, or thing, such as it is; or where the seller says openly or impliedly, "I know nothing of the goods, but from my invoice, and can take no risks," and the purchaser is clearly made to understand that he buys his commodity with all its faults.

To this it may be added, that the same exception is to be applied where positive municipal law, from any reason of legal policy, throws all risks upon the purchaser, and when the law is known and referred to, by the parties. No matter how unjust it might be in itself, as soon as the law thus indirectly makes a part of the contract, it affects the moral as well as the legal obligation. It must do so, since if thus taken into consideration, it will produce its effect, either in exciting greater diligence and caution; or else, the want of other security will be silently allowed for in the sale, by a diminution of price amounting to something like an informal insurance on the risk run. The law here, however, must not be merely known; the parties must also understand that they act in reference to it, before it has power thus to alter the prior obligations of reason and conscience.

This, by the way, is not ordinarily the case where the common law doctrine of sales and warranties, prevails.

In large commercial negotiations, among adroit and intelligent men of business, it may be so; but in common retail traffic the law is never thought of. When, in smaller matters, such a mistake happens, it is expected, as a thing of course, that it will be rectified, or allowed for; and if a mechanic or tradesman should think of refusing to do this, and of standing upon his legal rights, he would be looked upon as a knavish dealer, and most men would inflict on him the only punishment in their power—that of ceasing to be his customers.

Another important variation of circumstances occurs, where it is obvious that the buyer was not in fact influenced by the descriptions given, or by any expectation of a given kind or quality, but professedly meant to buy the specific thing, trusting wholly to his own judgment for its value and use.

Nor will the common rule hold good when the ascertaining the kind or quality of the thing sold does not depend upon a plain matter of fact, but rests on taste and opinion, so that the chance of error must be allowed by the buyer. Most of the fair sales of horses,—those where there is neither fraud nor any disease making the animal totally worthless—fall under one or other of these classes.

Cases arising out of the sale of works of art and taste are not uncommon in Europe, and are sometimes met with in our own country. The morality of such questions must frequently be settled on these last considerations.

For instance: I have an old picture which connoisseurs admire, and pronounce to be a Raphael. I send it to auction, and the auctioneer is authorized to state my opinion and belief of its excellence and originality. It is seen and examined; connoisseurs discuss its merits and genuineness, and one of them buys it at an immense price. Afterwards the true history of the picture is ascertained; or the opinion of great artists procured, when it turns out to be a second rate production.

Here, as a question of strict justice, there is no claim upon me to refund the price. It is true, that if I were a man of large fortune, and the buyer a poor picture-dealer, in point of liberality, generosity, and character, it would be morally right for me to relieve him from his bad purchase. But, if it be the poor picture-dealer who has sold to the man of fortune, the latter has no claim of right.

I mention this, by the way, to point out the importance of keeping the inquiry of strict justice wholly distinct from other moral considerations, and to show how apt our judgments are to run into confusion from neglecting this distinction.

With these exceptions, we may lay down the broad rule, that in every sale, or exchange, or purchase of services or of uses, (such as the hiring labour, or horses, or houses,) in short, in whatever human transactions *price* is concerned ;

The contract is not duly executed when the thing done, or delivered, varies materially in kind, or quality, from the kind or quality expressed between the parties, or understood by the one party, and known to be so understood by the other.

Kind and quality are expressed in a sale, not only by warranties and stipulations, or whatever else the law considers as making representations concerning them, but by all such words of description as are understood and are meant to be understood as describing the value, or sort, or degree of goodness of any thing offered for sale. They are implied, when from the known and avowed object of the buyer, they must be inferred of course as having been in the contemplation of the parties. They may also be implied from the price asked and accepted ; because any particular price fixed with reference to the market price, implies that the thing bought and sold possesses those qualities which create its ordinary demand.

With respect to the degree of variation that may be considered as *material*, as the shades of difference soften gradually into each other, the theoretical line of distinction cannot be very definitely and strongly marked. But, practically, there will be no great difficulty in deciding. If the variation relates to one of those common facts, (on which as we have seen, market price depends,) to be material, it must be such as, when known, to diminish its market price compared with other articles of the same name, and to give it a lower value in the estimation of all who deal in, or use such commodities.

It is also material when it so differs from the express and known understanding of both parties in making the bargain, that it is evident that had it been known, the buyer would not have bought, or would have bought at a lower rate. When we speak of buyer or seller, it is to be understood that the same reasoning applies, and the same facts are material to the contract of the letter and hirer; of the underwriter and the insured; with many others.

Perhaps it is scarcely necessary to add that a mutual mistake in the ownership of the thing sold, where the seller ignorantly sells what belonged to another, will for the same reasons discharge the buyer from his obligation, unless he had knowingly bought, not the thing itself, but the other's right, title, or claim to it.

The same reasonings and the same rules inverted will apply, where the error is against the interests of the seller. Such as where a silversmith sells a quantity of plated ware, and from ignorance or inadvertence delivers among it some solid silver plate of the same fashion. Such errors are far less common in trade than those of the opposite kind; because, however innocently mistakes regarding the nature and quality of wares may be made between subsequent buyers and sellers, they almost always originate in the fraud of the first seller or manufacturer, and are therefore, commonly, a substitution of inferior goods for more valuable.

When a contrary error does occur, it is clear that such delivery of a thing different in kind or quality from that intended, has no reference to the bargain actually concluded; provided that the difference does not arise from that deficiency of skill and judgment, the chances of which are always allowed. The seller has the goods, and the buyer has the price of them, but it is in consequence of a mistake, and not of a contract, for none has been made in reference to such goods. The mistake therefore ought to be rectified.

Thus it is, that while unjust concealment invalidates the bargain, honest mistakes and ignorance as to the intrinsic nature and quality of the thing sold, affect its execution. This distinction does not relate solely to the moral guilt or innocence of the parties; it also affects their rights, and varies their consequent duties.

Wilful concealment is of the nature of fraud. The offender is therefore bound in conscience, not only to rescind the bargain, or if it be too late for that, to make good the inequality; but also to remedy, to the best of his ability, all the injurious consequences which his wrong doing may have caused to him whom he has thus wronged. In the other case, it is a mutual mistake, without guilt or evil intention. Provided, then, there has been no gross negligence—for no man has the right to inflict the consequences of his own carelessness upon his neighbour—all that can be expected is, that neither should take advantage of the error at the other's expense.

If the bargain can be well executed, it must be; if this cannot be, each party must, as far as the worth of the thing goes, be placed in the situation they were in before the contract.

According to the circumstances of the case, either the contract, if not yet carried into effect, must be considered as at an end; or else the things delivered must be taken back, and others more exactly fulfilling the terms of sale, substituted; or the money must be paid back, and the goods received again; or, such compensation must be made for defects as may put the parties, as nearly as possible, upon their original footing.

If consequential damages ensue, they must be borne where they happen to fall; because there is no sufficient reason why of two innocent men one should be a loser rather than the other.

This distinction needs no proof, for it bears the evidence of truth and reason upon its face. It was recognised by the Roman jurists, and the ancient French Parliaments, and is acknowledged and applied in the present codes of France and Louisiana.

These rules which have been stated, are, I think, the just and sound moral laws of contracts, in relation to the suppression of facts, or insufficiency of price. They are deducible from the nature of things, and are consonant to our intuitive perceptions of right and wrong. Every man who will take the pains to analyze his own thoughts, will find, that they are involved in all the decisions he makes as to honesty and fair dealing in trade, and that they govern us at every moment in the little purchases of the markets, in the hiring or insuring of houses, the charge for personal or professional services, and all the detail of traffic, by which the business of life is carried on.

Much of the reasoning is so self-evident, that I have found it very difficult to avoid an air of common-place formality in stating and explaining methodically the principles which I have sought to establish. The only excuse for this is, that there is not one of them which has not been contradicted in some system of law or other, of the highest authority, and great practical influence. At the same time, it is no small corroboration of their truth, that every one of them is recognised in the most unanimous and unqualified judgments of public opinion upon personal character; and that there is not a single point of them which, on some occasion or other, judges and legislators have not recognised and enforced as a plain dictate of natural justice.

It now remains to inquire how far these principles are applicable to positive jurisprudence; and whether it be not possible, by confining and extending them wherever the law has already received them, and by rejecting all anomalous and contradictory rules and decisions, to make the ethics of public justice coincide throughout with the morality of private conscience.

CHAPTER VI.

Digression on the question; When, and how far, may positive law in administering justice between man and man, differ from the strict honesty and good faith required by conscience?

Legislators, lawyers, and moralists of all ages have agreed that there are some moral duties which it is not within the province of external human justice to enforce. These duties have been classed by moralists under the ill chosen name of duties of imperfect obligation. They are those which, like Benevolence, Gratitude, Liberality, are of their essence voluntary; the occasions, time, place, and manner of their exercise, their degree, their objects, must be left to the conscience or the sympathies of individuals. Obedience to them must be willing and cheerful, or it loses its moral nature. The external actions which they prompt or require are too infinitely diversified, and depend on too many and too secret considerations, to be reached by the laws of human wisdom; and can be judged only by him unto whom all hearts are open.

There is no difficulty in perceiving that, in respect to these virtues and duties, private conscience may, and ought to have one rule, and public Justice another.

But since the administration of Public Justice is instituted for the avowed purpose of rendering to every man his rights, and protecting him in the innocent enjoyment of them; since civil jurisprudence claims to be nothing more than the methodized and scientific knowledge of the just and unjust, it is a natural and important inquiry, when and wherefore it is that the law of personal morality and that of legal ethics can differ in regard to the requisitions of justice, of fair dealing, and of common honesty.

Can there be two sorts of honesty, and both legitimate? Or can positive legal enactment or judicial usage change that which is wrong into right?

These inquiries, taken in their whole extent, embrace the consideration of the fundamental right and policy of all those modifications of natural law, which positive legislation may justly make in relation to political rights, to crimes and punishments, to the tenure of real property, to the rules of descent, to the law of marriage, and of the other domestic relations.

This is far too wide a field of investigation to enter upon at present. Even in a limited view of the subject, with reference solely to the obligation of those reciprocal contracts relating to the transfer of property, it furnishes a theme for a volume rather than for a brief and hasty digression. Yet it will be useful, and I may almost say necessary, for our present purpose, to point out a few of the more obvious considerations which have a direct bearing upon the subject of this essay; as they indicate the only causes which can make it wise in policy, or justifiable in right, to modify and alter the rules of morals before applying them as the rules of law.

First of all, it is evident that it is possible for the rules of law to differ from those of conscience in regard to the same matter, in two ways. The law may either be in direct contradiction to private morality, so that one cannot be enforced without violating the other; or else it may differ merely in falling short of the requisitions of personal duty. In the one case the law is incompatible with that higher equity which is the true and only source of all valid law; in the other the imperfections of human wisdom and the impossibility of ascertaining the unuttered thoughts of man, and the true intention of parties, or some similar necessity of public policy may compel the judicial authority to withhold its aid from enforcing rights or remedying wrongs; whilst it still leaves the obligations of natural morality undisturbed and in full force.

Of this last and necessary difference the laws of all wise nations give many examples. Thus, in almost every regular and systematized administration of distributive justice, experience has proved that there is an exceedingly great difficulty in coming at the truth in controversies growing out of dealings which took place many years ago. Amongst other causes, this may arise from the death or removal of witnesses, the loss of written or other documentary evidence, and the uncertainty of memory. Public policy too was thought by sage and experienced legislators, to require, that for the peace of society and the security of property, some time should be fixed, after the lapse of which, litigation should be heard no longer; when the disputes and controversies of the father should cease to be visited upon the son, and every man might at length feel himself secure from dormant claims and long forgotten disputes. Hence, in most countries statutes of limitation or rules of prescription have been introduced, authoritatively assigning a certain number of years, after which the courts will not enforce a demand otherwise just, nor give compensation for any injury to person or character, however serious. Meanwhile the law does not venture to interfere to change the personal obligations between the parties; it only for other reasons declines giving them their customary legal effect.

But if the law had proclaimed that after six years neglect of claiming your due, your debtor should not only be released from his debt, but that he and his heirs should have the right of recovering it back from you at any time, in case he had paid you from conscientious motives; or if it were enacted that the debtor should be subject to some penalty if he made such a payment, here would be an extravagant and inexcusable violation of justice. No one doubts that such direct contradictions to natural equity are on the very face of them tyrannical, oppressive, and contrary to the primary purposes of society.

Unless some reasonable cause be shown, the refusal of the sovereign, or the judicial power, to grant justice, is palpably as inexcusable as the actual perpetration of positive injustice. By suffering wrong to be done with impunity, they allow and sanction it. The main object of society being the protection of private rights, public justice is bound to guard and enforce them to the best of its ability. Hence it closely follows that the law is to be justified in falling short of the dictates of natural justice, and in refusing to enforce what good faith decrees, solely by NECESSITY.

Wherever and whenever the law, without this excuse, permits one citizen to enjoy that, which if he were an honest man he would resign to his neighbour, the great end of all law is so far frustrated.

The FIRST and most frequent form of that necessity which constitutes a valid ground for the administration of justice to vary *positive law*, from the supreme law of a pure and enlightened conscience, is *that necessity which arises from the imperfections of human evidence.*

The danger of mistake, as well as of wilful falsehood, is so great; and even where the veracity of the witness is unsuspected, it is so difficult to deduce from the exterior facts of conduct, and language, the real intentions of men; and words themselves are so vague and lax in their significations, that human justice is obliged to lay down certain general and fixed rules, and to confess, that it is unable to decide with precision on particular cases, except within these bounds. Hence have arisen those terms of limitation of actions, and prescription in rights, which have just been mentioned. Hence, too, since it is by no means easy to distinguish between a thoughtless declaration of intention, and a deliberate promise calculated to mislead the receiver, the common and the civil law have agreed in refusing to sustain any action for the breach of a naked promise to do or give any thing upon one side without any compensation, given or stipulated upon the other. Their maxim is that a bare promise without a consideration, will not support an action; *ex nudo pacto, non oritur actio.* Not that an honest man must not consider himself bound by the expectation which he intentionally and deliberately excited in another, in some moment of generosity; but no action is entertained on such a promise, because it is thought that this would lead to endless litigation, while the proof of the real intention of the promiser, would be liable to the greatest misrepresentation and abuse.

A similar uncertainty caused the enactment of the Statute of Frauds, and the analogous provisions in the laws or usages of Rome, of France, and Holland. On this ground the law of England has refused to admit any action, to charge the defendant for the debt or default of a third person, unless the agreement be in writing, and signed by the party; and has pronounced that, "no contract for the sale of goods, wares, and merchandise for more than a certain price shall be good, unless accompanied by delivery in part, or payment of earnest, or some written memorandum of the bargain."

So too, in the French law, all verbal evidence whatever is excluded in certain kinds of contracts; and in these peculiar instances no recovery can be had, unless the demand be supported by written, and sometimes by notarially certified proof.

In each and all of the cases falling under these provisions, it is clear that the duty of one party, and the claim in conscience of the other, remain unchanged; whilst at the same time the law may be wise in policy and justifiable in equity, in refusing to enforce either ; since this cannot be done in any single instance, unless at the hazard of committing injustice in many others.

It is a whimsical but shrewd remark of some wit, that when a Frenchman and an Englishman agree in opinion about any thing whatever, it is certain that they must both be right. The agreement of the policy of so great a part of Europe in so many of these limitations of justice, strongly proves their wisdom. But that wisdom is no other than the perception of a common necessity.

Nevertheless, if these limitations were arbitrary or capricious, or if originally founded in necessity, changes in the state of society and manners should make them needless, they would then become imperfections disgraceful to any civilized community. Disgraceful imperfections do I term them?—they would then be a violation of that solemn pledge which the rulers of every nation are bound to give to its citizens—*Nulli negabimus, nulli differemus justitiam et rectum ;* All shall have right and justice freely and completely—without denial and without delay. Thus speaks Magna Charta, and so it is re-echoed in our own state constitutions and Bills of Rights. Far above this, it is a duty that needs no human sanction. It is the universal and unchanging mandate of that law written by God's own hand on the hearts of all men.

But there is a SECOND cause which may often fairly and properly vary the rule of legal right, from that of right in conscience. This may be termed the necessity of public policy. The line of distinction between this and the former species of necessity is not always very clear, so that they often run into each other. There are many contracts between man and man, which may be fair in themselves, but in some way or other, have a farther bearing, and involve, directly or remotely, the interests of others. There may, too, be sound reasons of state policy, with which, when private rights come in collision, the latter must give way. Individuals must not only transact *bona fide* between themselves, but they must not make such bargains, nor make them in such a manner, as to be injurious to other persons, who stand in a relation to be affected by the contract or its consequences. Where some of the rest of mankind are concerned besides the parties, public utility has a right to impose new restrictions for the common protection.* Besides this, there are many concerns, wherein it is almost a matter of indifference, by what rule they are regulated, and yet it is absolutely necessary that they should be positively regulated in some one way. These must then be governed by arbitrary general laws, that the citizen may be apprized of his rights and duties.

* The subject of the propriety of courts being governed by reasons of public utility, and the extent of the doctrine is touched upon briefly, but with his usual ability and wisdom, by Lord Chancellor Hardwicke, in the great case of the Earl of Chesterfield *v.* Sir Abraham Jansen, 2 Vesey, 155.

Thus, among many equally convenient modes of business, there must be some positive preference of one to another, some unvarying law as to the forms and methods, and effects of obligations. For example. In the law of promissory notes and bills of exchange, the legislative and judicial authority have not only to look at what may be just as between any two immediate parties to such a negotiation, but also, for the sake of the whole commercial community, to establish by well-settled rules, the mode and effect of endorsement and acceptance, and discharge of acceptance, and of notice, and protest with the various other incidents of negotiable paper.

Every one who knows any thing of this head of the law merchant will admit the wisdom and justice of such regulations; and yet the slightest acquaintance with the actual business of life, will suggest to our minds various cases, when it would be basely dishonest for a party to such paper to take advantage of that discharge from legal responsibility, which the interests of commerce made it necessary and just that the law should provide, under certain circumstances, as a general rule.

Thus, too, with respect to real estate and mortgages, nothing can be more plain than the contract between the mortgagor and mortgagee; but what public policy may require, for the prevention of frauds, and the protection of *bona fide* purchasers or subsequent mortgagees, is another question. This may require legislative provisions or judicial regulations. But these, from the imperfection of all human laws, may sometimes leave the ignorant and innocent without any relief, except what he can find in the honour and voluntary good faith of him whom he has trusted.

The policy of the State may also interfere in private contracts, for reasons purely national and political: as in regard to the revenue laws, and those regulating shipping and navigation, or where stamp duties are imposed, for the purpose of taxation, on notes, deeds, or wills.* Where the state thus requires, for its own interests, registers, certificates, stamps, &c. it becomes, as it were, a third party to every contract in which they are used, and is compelled to debar from their legal rights all who

* The English decisions on sailor's sales of their prize-money suggests another apposite illustration of this subject. In Baldwin *v.* Rockford, 1 Wilson, 299, a case decided some fifty years ago, two sailors having assigned their shares of prize-money for half their worth, the Chancellor, (Lord Camden,) relieved them against the assignment, chiefly, it seems, from that strong presumptive evidence of unfair advantage having been taken, which arises from the general character of sailors; " for, he said, there could not be a more useful set of men to the public, nor a more unthinking set of people than common sailors; who, as soon as ever they get on shore, for the sake of a little immediate pleasure, are willing to part with their right to any thing in expectancy, for a little in possession; and, accordingly, the law considering them as not fit to take care of themselves, takes care of them, against themselves." The Chancellor was, I presume, right. But, supposing, what it requires no great excess of sanguine philanthropy to believe, that that extension of knowledge, which is the best characteristic of our age should, in the course of another generation, make the sailors of England as prudent and shrewd a body of men as the Scotch mechanics, or the sailors of some of the eastern parts of the United States, would not the application of this rule serve as an inducement to fraud, and be a real oppression and injustice to those whom it was instituted to serve?

refuse to comply with these requisitions. Notwithstanding this, in private conscience, these rights remain unimpaired.

Between this necessity of public utility, and the principle of limitation arising from defective evidence, may be placed a third class, comprehending a number of common and useful rules of law varying from natural justice. Many of these cases may be assigned to either former head; as in fact most of the cases of either class may rather be distinguished than divided from one another. By these last are meant those prohibitory or preventive rules of policy, intended to suppress certain immoral or injurious practices, or to protect particular classes of society. Such regulations, prudent in themselves, are necessarily very general; and by that generality, may be occasionally the means of working injustice.

With this view, it is wisely settled as a rule of judicial policy, that the trustee, the assignee, the executor, the commissioner, shall not be permitted to buy his trust property on his own account; and such a sale would be held invalid, though made with the purest intentions. This is meant as a preventive to hinder the trustee from being tempted to betray his duty. It may also be considered as a rule of evidence, because without some such general prohibition, where all the evidence must be in the hands of the trustee, it would be impossible for the courts to get at the facts necessary to relieve the ward or the orphan against any iniquity, however gross.

The protection which the laws of most civilized countries afford to minors, presents another example slightly varied in its circumstances, resting partly on the necessity of a very general rule of evidence, partly upon considerations of public policy. It is most salutary in itself, yet subject to be abused to fraudulent purposes.

The probability is so strong, that a youth, gay, sanguine, ardent, confiding, and ignorant of the ways of men, and the modes of business, will be cheated in all bargains beyond those which his daily support and comfort require and accustom him to make; and the suppression of all evidence regarding such transaction is so easy for any veteran rogue into whose snare he may fall, that the law has in most ages and countries determined to refuse enforcing any such agreement; leaving the whole matter to the honour of the young, and the prudence of those who deal with them.

Upon the same ground the laws of many nations have extended this sort of protection to other classes of society, as in various countries, to married women, and in England, both by statute and by judicial decisions, to sailors. The wisdom of these exemptions may be, and has been doubted; and if they are not necessary, they are wrong.

Whenever, and for whatsoever reason the Law

thus substitutes for the natural and immediate conclusions of reason, the more refined and enlarged considerations of political wisdom, it is meant, and in all really wise legislation it for the most part happens, that these positive requisitions of law become known to most of those whom they concern. Thus all private arrangements and agreements are made with reference to them. Then, the rule of conscience and that of the law become the same. It is we know a dictate of natural reason, that no man should undertake to sell what he does not know to belong to him, and therefore, the seller impliedly warrants the right of property. If the thing sold turns out to belong to a third person, the seller must make it good. Yet there may possibly be very sufficient reason of public utility, why in some kinds of property the law should change this rule, and declare that the courts should grant no relief to an unfortunate purchaser, except the seller had given him a written warranty of title. If this were the law, and so understood at the time of purchase, the contract is varied by it, and the seller, in good faith, is as much discharged from the loss in conscience, as he is in law.

But the right, the single and only ground of right, for Law-makers, whether in the senate or on the bench, to interfere in this manner, rests in necessity. Whenever public utility has no urgent reason for this interference, the right itself falls to the ground.

The artificial rule of law may be officially promulgated and even generally known. Still, as long as it is not known to all, there is a great hazard that it will sometimes work injustice. If so, this is a useless positive evil, to which there is no countervailing benefit.

The self-same considerations mark out clearly not only when this interference may justly take place, but also, how far it may go. If the positive regulations are few and simple, and drawn from the actual usages of society, and in conformity with our modes of thoughts and habits of business, they soon become well known; not certainly to all—but to all who have much occasion to use them. They then enter silently into all negotiations, they make a real, as well as a technical part of them, and thus positive law and natural justice coincide.

The law-merchant of the modern civilized world, as to negotiable paper, affords admirable example of this. Among millions of daily transactions, there but now and then occurs an instance where the parties were not sufficiently aware of their legal rights and responsibilities, and where the courts by applying the rule of law would not in fact execute the true intentions and undertakings of the maker, acceptor, or endorser.

But if a little of the artificial reasoning and technical subtilties of the common law doctrine of real estate, had been at an early period introduced into this branch of the law-merchant.—and it would have needed nothing but a little ingenuity, and the sanction of one or two venerable names to have done it—the negotiation of a bill of exchange would have become as mysterious and technical an affair as a deed of trusts and settlements; no unprofessional man could have told what his precise engagements and responsibilities were; while courts, in innumerable instances, would cease to administer justice, and would afford protection to fraud.

Thus we come to the broad conclusion that the law can never justly and wisely vary from the rule of private honesty, unless when the necessity of public good requires it, and then so far, and no farther than that necessity demands. Great men have told us that it is of special little consequence what the law is, provided it be certain. Its provisions, say they, become known, and men govern themselves accordingly. This is not true.

No matter how certain and precise the law may be, if in its intention it be a capricious and useless departure from the rule which unaided common sense would prescribe to an intelligent individual; or if in aiming at a reasonable and justifiable ultimate object, it uses, as the means, regulations abhorrent to the usages or even to the prejudices of the people, or unnecessarily formal, technical, and remote from the reason of common life, then the law never becomes known to those whose affairs it regulates.

The crafty and knavish do know it, and they use it for their own ends. The simple and the ignorant are injured, and can find no redress. The contrast between technical sense and common sense becomes harassing and perplexing to all. There is one rule of honesty with our baker and butcher, and another in the stock exchange, the horse-market, and the courts. The law loses public confidence, and its ministers their just title to respect. The courts of justice are crowded and oppressed with a mass of litigation, from questions which in a simpler jurisprudence would never have arisen. Fraud often triumphs over honesty; but the better sense and the better feeling of mankind cannot always be perverted, and in hard and extreme cases, judges sometimes, and juries oftener, will bend or break the law to their own irresistible notions of equity. Thus finally vanishes that very certainty, which is so boldly lauded as an adequate substitnte for justice.

Every unnecessary deviation in law from what is just in morals, is unjust. Yet such is the force of early prejudice, that great jurists who have been able and eloquent in inculcating the natural supremacy of equity and reason, over positive rules and irrational customs, and who while they have evinced a profound knowledge of the philosophy of jurisprudence, have been most skilful in its practical application, have conceded that legal systems without better foundation than precedent and accident, may be as useful as any, though less pleasing to the student, and less beautiful in the scholar's eye.

"If law," says Sir William Jones, "be a science, and deserves that sublime name, it must be founded in principle, and claim an exalted rank in the empire of reason. But if it be merely an unconnected series of decisions, its use may remain though its dignity be lessened."*

The first position is worthy of the noble spirit and sound intellect of this wise and high-principled lawyer. But if the law of any nation be "merely an unconnected series of decisions," its use does not, and cannot remain. It ceases to be the remedy of the injured, and the shield of the weak. To the ignorant it becomes a snare, but a weapon to the wrongdoer.

Lord Mansfield has termed Socrates "the great lawyer of antiquity; since," said he, "the principles of all law are founded in philosophy."† The philosophy which Socrates taught, and where Mansfield sought for the principles of jurisprudence, was that of common sense and moral reason. Nor can the law fulfil its true uses, if it rests

* Sir W. Jones. Law of Bailment.

† It is a phrase used by Lord Mansfield in his Eulogy upon Lord Hardwicke, contained in an answer to the address of the members of Lincoln's Inn, upon his promotion to the bench. I know of no short prose composition in our language, so exquisite for the irregular melody of its pure and idiomatic English. It has the higher merit of eulogizing a great man, and a rival in fame, with the reverent admiration of kindred genius.

upon any other basis. Place it upon any other foundation, and what is it? A system whose language, reasons, and distinctions, are totally dark and mysterious to all but those whose daily business it is to study them,—very imperfectly comprehended by the most of these; natural and beautiful to none but a few antiquarian rabbis. All its doctrines, axioms, maxims, and adages, become malleable to the caprice of the bench. They are flexible in the hand of the judge upon whom public opinion is no check, and whose reasoning is unintelligible to all but the bar.

Meanwhile, the honest man is every moment entrapped from presuming that the rules of right and wrong are also the rules of justice in the courts. Worse than this, the law which should be the guardian of morals, becomes the teacher of dishonesty. The careless, the ignorant, all on whom pure religion or high honour have little hold, are suffered every hour to imbibe from the lessons of the law the spirit of low, evasive, dishonourable, and dishonest dealing.

To conclude, the doctrines of sound legal ethics, and those of a strict and enlightened private honesty, must always run together, except so far as the former are modified by necessity. Some of the causes of that necessity I have attempted to point out as existing in considerations of public policy, or in the imperfection of human evidence. There are perhaps a few others. It is a field of inquiry which I have ventured to explore hastily and without a guide. The philosophy of the subject has never, I believe, been formally investigated, and it is worthy of the genius of a Montesquieu.

CHAPTER VII.

The applicability of the rules of natural justice to the law of contracts, shewn from the experience afforded by their partial adoption in the law of Insurance—In Equity—and in the Civil Law.

KEEPING steadily in view this fundamental truth, that it can never be either right or wise for civil tribunals to establish rules of justice varying from those pronounced by the tribunal of conscience, unless, when compelled by absolute necessity or clear public utility; let us next proceed to inquire whether any such valid reason exists, why the morality of contracts should not also be in substance their external law.

I dare to assert without hesitation, and that in contradiction to much, and high, and venerable authority, that there is no such sufficient reason; that the rules of strict honesty regarding inequality of knowledge or of price, and those of uninstructed common sense as to the interpretation and execution of bargains, can be, and therefore ought to be, the governing principles of the whole law of contracts.

It is true that courts must be directed in the application of these as well as of most other correct doctrines of legal ethics, as well as restricted in the remedies they furnish, by necessary regulations of limitation as to time and person, of uniformity of decision, of commercial usage, and by positive rules of evidence. But there can be no other justifiable exceptions. The evident matter of fact demonstration of the applicability of these principles to the science of law, and of their practical fitness for the concerns of life, is to be seen in the plain facts, that amidst many contradictions and anomalies, they are to be found recognised and extensively acted upon, in various parts of the law of England, of the United States, and of the continent of Europe—that wherever they have been so applied, those heads or titles of the law, where they are recognised, have not only been pre-eminent for their clearness, certainty, and legal consistency, but have received the unanimous approbation of intelligent men of business; have been most generally understood and acted upon by that portion of the community to whose concerns they relate; and after having once been legislatively or judicially promulgated, have furnished the least room for doubtful litigation, or for fraudulent advantages over the honourable and confiding.

On the other hand, uniform experience has shown, that whatsoever doctrines or decisions on the law of Sales, or of the analogous kinds of contracts, are anomalous and contradictory to these; however well known they may become to lawyers, and well settled in the courts, they never have been comprehended by the great mass of those whose daily concerns they regulate, but have ever been to them a mystery and a difficulty, ever fruitful in litigation, and in successful trick.

Moreover, it is very seldom true in fact, that legal doctrines of this character are well settled in the courts, or received without doubt or uncertainty among the mass of the legal profession. Countries, or states, or provinces, recognising the same system of arbitrary law, vary in the degree to which they receive and apply special points of it. Juries and inferior courts are in constant collision with the higher dignitaries of the law; and even in the superior tribunals, times, occasions, the accidental personal character of judges, or the prevailing studies and opinions of the day, bend the rule and its meaning and application sometimes one way, and then again the other.

They are the arbitrary inventions of men; and to such variations are all man's inventions inevitably doomed. Truth alone is immutable and eternal.

It is very generally conceded, that if there is any part of our jurisprudence rational, wise, consistent, easily referrible to first principles, combining happily the necessary uniformity of human laws with exact justice in each individual case, it is the law of Insurance.

Whilst by far the greater part of our law is perfectly incomprehensible to all but those whose daily study it is; and while men act as trustees or agents, and buy and sell ships or houses, and hold and sell real estate, for half their lives, without ever hoping to comprehend the precise limits and reasons of their rights and duties; our law of Insurance is, in the main, level to the comprehension, and will command the assent, of every one who can read and think. All whose special business relates to insurance, may, and many do, become acquainted with its doctrines, and know enough of it for the common uses of business.

It has another and peculiar praise. Insurance law is not simply a branch of the law of England, or of the United States. It is a part of the law of the sea. It belongs to the Law Merchant of the world. The decisions of Mansfield, and of the English and American judges who have followed the lights of his guiding mind, are law at Paris, Amsterdam, and Hamburg, as well as at New-York and New-Orleans.

Now, it is remarkable that on this head of our jurisprudence, whose equity and wisdom have been confessed and admired by lawyers and merchants of all nations, every rule and principle of the doctrine of contracts which have been stated in these pages, as being those of honesty and fair dealing in private concerns, is to be found either actually and formally laid down as the legal rule, or practically recognised in the decisions, as being such.

It was stated as a sound general rule, for our moral conduct in contracts and sales, that "No advantage can be fairly taken in a bargain or sale, from the suppression of any fact, materially and of course, affecting that ordinary estimate which fixes the market value of the subject of the contract; and regarding which, the fact of the bargain alone proves that it was presumed, by the losing party, that no such advantage would be taken."

The brief view of the doctrine of insurance, already given in the second chapter of this essay, is quite sufficient to show the perfect consonancy between the law of insurance, and this rule. A policy is adjudged to be void wherever either party is misled, or is not enabled to make a fair estimate of the value of the risk; that is to say, such an estimate as any other judicious underwriter, under similar circumstances, might make from a view of the known facts. This may be caused either by misrepresentation or by concealment of *material* facts. By a fact material to the risk is meant one which shows the nature and extent of the risk, one which would of necessity influence the mind of an underwriter in determining whether he would insure at all, or at what premium. A concealment is defined to be the suppression or reservation of some such fact, within the knowledge of either party, and which the other has not the means of knowing, or is presumed not to know.*

The French law here exactly agrees with the English and our own. It declares that, "any concealment, any misrepresentation, on the part of the insured, any variation between the contract of insurance and the bill of lading, which would lessen the estimation of the risk, or change the subject of it, annuls the insurance."†

A merchant having intelligence of a storm in the Baltic, where many vessels were lost, among which he has reason, from dates and circumstances, to believe, is one of his own, insures his ship without communicating this news. Here, the courts of Washington and Westminster would agree with those of the *Palais* at Paris, that the policy was void. The known danger of the ship is a fact necessarily and materially entering into the common estimate of the risk with all underwriters in their calculation of the fair premium upon such a risk.

* The reasons and authorities for all these points may be found in the excellent work of our countryman, Philips, on Insurance, c. vii. and in the corresponding sections of Marshall and Park's well known books on the same subject.

† "Toute reticence, toute fausse déclaration de la part de l'assuré, toute différence entre le contrat d'assurance et le connaissement, qui diminurarient l'opinion du risque ou en changeraient le sujet, annullent l'assurance." Code de Commerce, art. 348.

The underwriting, at the rate it was done, proves, that no such danger was known, and that the insurer must have presumed that no advantage would be taken of any secret knowledge on the subject.

So again: If a vessel is known to be out of time, (as the phrase is,) that fact must be told, or the policy is void. The reason Lord Chief Justice Kenyon assigns for it, is, "because premiums sustain a considerable advance when a ship is deemed a missing ship."* What does this mean, but that the fact of a ship being a "missing ship" or not, enters materially, and of course into the common estimate which fixes the rate of premium, and therefore must not be concealed?

In examining the precise limits of this principle, it was stated as the converse of the last rule, and in some sort an inference from it, that—"There is nothing unfair in using any superior sagacity as to probabilities, or in applying greater skill and knowledge as to those facts which do not necessarily enter into the general calculation of those who fix the current price, or concerning which no confidence express or implied is reposed."

This rule cannot receive a better comment or clearer illustration than is to be found in the reasoning of Lord Mansfield, in deciding the famous case of Carter *v.* Boehm,† which definitely settled the law of insurance in this respect.

* McAndrews *v.* Bell, 1 Esp. 373.
† 3 Burrows, 1905.

"Good faith, says he, forbids either party, by con-
"cealing what he knows, to draw the other into a
"bargain, from his ignorance of that fact, and his
"believing the contrary. The keeping back such
"circumstance is a fraud, and although the sup-
"pression should happen through mistake, the po-
"licy is void, because the risk is different from that
"understood and intended to be run.

"The insured need not mention what the under-
"writer knows, or what way soever he came by that
"knowledge, or what he ought to know, or takes
"upon himself the knowledge of, or waives being
"informed of; or what lessens the risk, or every
"cause which may occasion natural perils, as the
"difficulty of the voyage, kind of seasons, probabi-
"lity of hurricanes, earthquakes, &c.; nor every
"cause which may occasion political perils, from the
"rupture of states, from war and the various opera-
"tion of it, nor the probability of safety from
"the continuance or return of peace, or the inability
"of the enemy. Men argue differently from natu-
"ral phenomena, and the means of information and
"judging are open to both; each professes to act
"on his own skill and sagacity. The rule is adapt-
"ed to *facts* which are privately known to one par-
"ty, and which the other is ignorant of, or has no
"reason to suspect."

Again: I have considered it as clear in the light of common sense, though legal sense has doubted and debated about the matter—"that there is no such thing, of itself, without reference to other considerations, as inadequacy of price, and therefore that every price fairly settled without mistake as to facts, is a fair price." Now this is the universal understanding of underwriters and merchants as to insurance. If the competition of insurance companies should reduce the premiums* to the lowest possible rate, far beneath the chance of any profit from the business, still the underwriters have just reason to complain. They have consented to take the premiums, no matter how inadequate to the risk, and are bound in conscience, as well as law, to take their chance and to pay their losses.

But it was added, that there is another view of inadequacy of price, in which "a price much greater or less than things perfectly similar could be bought or sold for, at the time, may afford strong presumptive evidence of fraud or mistake." This distinction, though not laid down in words, is impliedly recognised in the law of insurance. The rate of premium, though a matter in itself quite indifferent to the validity of the policy, may yet be a most important circumstance in cases of doubt in determining whether a fair representation has been made. If the risk appears to have been known by the assured to be extraordinary, whilst he offered and gave

* This is the fact in the city of New-York at the moment I am now writing, as to marine insurance, and in a less degree also as to fire.

but an ordinary premium for the voyage, a strong presumption arises that the representation of facts could not have been fair.* Upon the same principle, an extraordinary premium paid is good ground for presuming that the risk was represented as more than common.†

Another prominent point of the natural law regarding contracts has been stated to be, "that contracts are not duly executed, when the thing done or delivered varies materially in kind or quality from those expressed between the parties, or understood by the one party, and known by the other to be so understood."

This is applied in the most unqualified manner in insurance. It is on this very ground that a misrepresentation made through mistake or oversight, releases the underwriter from the obligation of his policy. "Though the suppression should happen through mistake," says Lord Mansfield, "the policy is void, because the risk is different from that understood, and intended to be run."‡

Moreover, in insurance the law always implies a warranty of the sea-worthiness of the vessel, from the very fact of her being insured. The insurer is freed from his contract, if the ship is rotten, or her iron work decayed, or loose, or her original con-

* Bridges *v.* Hunter, 1. Maule and Selwyn, 19.

† Freeland *v.* Glover, 7 East, 457

‡ 3 Burrows, 1906

struction grossly defective as to strength, or if she has not the usual sea-stores on board, the customary sails, tackle, cables and anchors, or if she is not manned with a competent crew. And all this is warranted without a word actually passing on the subject.

Here there is no rule of *caveat emptor*. The fact of assuming a risk at a given and usual price, is held legally (as a fair price in all purchases ought to be held,) to afford sufficient evidence that it was supposed or presumed that the subject of the contract had the ordinary qualities which fit it for the common uses of such things.

Here then the whole argument might be safely rested. The striking fact that the plain rules of conscience and moral honesty have been universally adopted as the legal rules in this class of contracts, evinces, that this is practicable as to all cases, and that there is no reason whatever, whether of judicial necessity, or of public policy, to make them vary from each other.

If there is no impediment arising from the nature of the transaction and the difficulty of the proof of the facts, sufficient to hinder their adoption in such contracts, there cannot well be in any other. As to mere matters of fact, if we consider the complication of circumstances, the difficulty of ascertaining them, and the uncertainty of opinion which may take place regarding the condition and character of the vessel, the kind and value of goods, the variety of risks insured against, and of events which affect a policy, and the great number of interests and parties which may be immediately or indirectly embraced in it; we must confess that an ordinary marine insurance is a far more complicated transaction than almost any that fall under the law of sales or of mutual contracts.

In addition to this complication of facts, the effect of a policy is, moreover, influenced and altered by political considerations, by war and peace, by the laws of nations,—yet more by the arbitrary interpretation and application of that law, and finally, by local regulations of revenue and police, and quarantine laws abroad. The first marine policy which one would meet with, will probably involve more points of law and fact, than one out of a thousand of any other kind of contract.

Nor has the escaping or avoiding these difficulties been owing to the superior caution and accuracy of those who carry on this business. This might have been reasonably expected to have been the case; but the fact is not so. There are few formal bargains in which a far more exact and technical precision is not to be found in the instruments or memorandums of them. "A policy of insurance," have said some of the most learned judges of England, "is an obscure, incoherent, and very strange instrument."* Nor has this instrument much improved in the United States.— "Policies of insurance, says Chief Justice Marshall, are generally the most informal instruments brought into courts of justice."†

What is it then that has given so great a degree of certainty to this loose and inaccurate instrument, and made it to preserve a uniform construction, at the same time that it is interpreted so as ordinarily to express the true intent of the parties? It is the interpreting and enforcing it by legal principles consonant to the usages of commerce, the common sense of men of business, and the moral nature of all.

Thus the law of insurance alone proves that there is no reason why the principles of sound morals might not be applied universally to the law of contracts. It does more. It proves that as a mere question of policy they ought to be so applied. For there is no title of our law so perfectly answering the end and object of scientific law, so fairly distributing justice, and giving so little shelter to fraud. Indeed fraud has there no shelter, unless it resort to the desperate and hazardous resource of forgery and perjury. At the same time there is nothing to be found there romantic or impracticable, or in any

* It is so described by Judge Buller, and by Ch. Just. Sir James Mansfield, 4 T. R. 210. 4 Taunton, 380. Judge Lawrence says, in 3 East, 673, "it is wonderful that policies should be drawn with such laxity."

† 5 Cranch, 342.

wise inconsistent with the interests and policy of commerce. And if it is still imperfect or doubtful in some few points, if it contains some real or apparent antinomies and contradictions, these are unquestionably not to be ascribed to any error or obscurity in its fundamental doctrines, but wholly to the circumstance that they have been administered and applied by judges and lawyers, who upon all other subjects are in the constant habit of arguing upon far other principles, and of pronouncing the decisions of a law whose general rules have nothing in common with those of this particular branch of it. Hence has naturally occurred an occasional intrusion of the common law-spirit into the law of insurance, naturally producing some little confusion in a few questions, though much less, and much more seldom than occurs in any other part of our legal institutions.

There is no other part of the law in which these doctrines are so uniformly recognised and applied. The policy and genius of the old common law of contracts is in hostility to them. Yet without being formally enunciated as legal rules, they have silently made their way; case after case has been decided in conformity with them, and thence have been formed the most valuable parts of the English equity system.

It is now well settled law in the English chancery, and in the several courts of equity jurisdiction in the United States, that the trustee or assignee must not use the superiority afforded by his situation of confidence to buy or sell for his own benefit; that in contracts between parent and child, the parent commits a legal fraud, if he turns to his own account the confidence flowing from filial affection; that the confidence impliedly reposed by the ward in his guardian is as inviolable; and that the same principle holds good as to all advantages gained by means of any confidence growing out of the peculiar relations of the parties.*

Wherever equity thus interferes, it does no more than literally enforce that fundamental rule, the observation of which has been stated as essential to good faith in all contracts: "that it is not permitted in conscience to take advantage, in any respect, where it is presumed by the one side, and understood to be so presumed by the other, that no advantage would be taken." To this broad foundation must be referred a multitude of these

* As to the relation of trustees and their trustors, see Fox *v.* Mackreth, 2 Brown, Ch. C. 400; 4 Brown, P. C 258; 5 Vesey, 678; 6 Vesey, 627; 8 Vesey, 337, settled by Lords Thurlow, Alvanley, and Eldon. In America the same principles have been wisely and ably applied and enforced by Chancellor Kent, in Green *v.* Winter, 1 Johns. Chan. Rep. 27; Pasket *v.* Alexander, 1 John. C. R. 394; also, 4 John. C. R. 303; 5 Johns. Ch. R. 497, & 7 Johns. C. R. 174.—Regarding the abuse of confidence, between Parent *v.* Child, see 1 Ves. 400; between Guardian & Ward. 1 P Wms. 121; 2. Vesey, 547; between Attorney and Client, 2 Atkyns 25, 4 Bro. Ch. R. 350; and between Master and Servant; 5 Vesey, 87. All of the older cases on this branch of equity are collected and arranged under their several heads, in the case of Fox *v.* Mackreth, 2 Bro. C. C. 400, so frequently above referred to.

decisions, each of which, singly, may have appeared to rest on some more narrow and partial considerations.

Again: In many cases, some few of which have been briefly recapitulated in a former chapter,* equity has pronounced, that "the suppression of truth not less than the insinuation of falsehood, is good ground to set aside a conveyance, or release;"† and that "wilful concealment of the truth on a material point by one party, made to keep the other in ignorance to profit thereby, will be considered as a gross fraud, and good ground to set aside the contract."‡

Whoever will patiently examine these decisions, (which it would be tedious and useless to detail in this place,) will find in every one of them, that the material facts concealed were precisely those which "necessarily enter into the common estimate of price;" and that the fraud is no other than the breach of an implied confidence, by taking an advantage where the bargain went upon an understood presumption, that no advantage was to be taken.

Moreover, equity has, under peculiar circumstances, so far broken in upon the strict common law notions of sales, and its unconscientious maxim

* See chap. ii. p. 50, 53.

† Broderick *v.* Broderick, 1 P. W. 239. 2 Bro. C. C. 150.

‡ See 2 Powell on Contracts, 203, and the cases there cited.

of *caveat emptor*, as to permit the defendant to show, by any evidence, that the contract insisted on by the plaintiff, did not embrace the real meaning of the bargain, and to prove, even in opposition to a formal and written instrument, that "this was not the agreement intended to be signed;" that there was some mistake or omission, which made the written agreement vary from the bargain in contemplation. "There is no doubt," said Lord Chancellor Hardwicke, in a case of this nature, "that this defence ought to be received, "and it is quite equal whether it is insisted on as "a mistake, or as a fraud."* Since his time, such mistakes have afforded a frequent ground of defence in equity, which has always been sustained by the courts.†

What is this but an implied admission in a few peculiar cases, of what has been stated as the sound general rule in all, (and I can see no reason to limit it,) that, "no contract is duly executed when the thing done, or delivered, varies materially in kind or quality, from those understood between the parties?"

There is yet another point, whereon numerous Chancery decisions correspond with our doctrines. It has been said, that inadequacy of price is in itself an unreal notion, unless by comparison

* Joynes *v.* Stathan, 3 Atk. 397.

† 6 Vesey, 328. 1 Schoale and Lefroy, 39, &c.

of the price agreed on with the current price at which the same or similar things could be procured by, or from others, there arises a presumptive evidence that the bargain was made under some gross delusion. Now, in spite of numerous contradictions, and a multitude of anomalous cases, the prevailing doctrine is that stated by Lord Eldon: "Unless inadequacy of price amounts, in itself, to conclusive and decisive evidence of fraud in the transaction, it is not a sufficient ground for refusing a specific performance."*

Nor is it in Equity or Insurance law only, that we can find proof of the utility, and even the necessity of the adoption of these principles, in the administration of justice. There is one very remarkable class of cases in the common law courts, relating to the payment of forged bank notes, or negotiable paper, and all that passes current for money, where the buyer and seller are in mutual ignorance of the forgery. As money and such paper are personal property, transferable on delivery, the passing of them is nothing but a sale or exchange of them for goods. To preserve the uniformity and analogy of the law, they too should be included under the common law rules, and the doctrine of *caveat emptor*. But the law has been settled on precisely the opposite principle. One of the first modern cases

* 9 Vesey, 246.

on this point was decided in the Supreme Court of New-York, and Kent, then Chief Justice, in delivering the opinion of the court, admits, without the least limitation, the justice of the civil law rule of sales, which is the same, substantially, with that which I have considered as being the sound rule of moral obligation. "The justice of the case," says he, "is clearly with the defendant. He part-"ed with his goods without receiving the compen-"sation which was intended. It would be matter "of regret if the law obliged us to regard a pay-"ment in counterfeit instead of genuine bank "bills, as a valid payment of debt, merely because "the creditor did not perceive and detect the false "bills, at the time of payment. The reasonable "doctrine, and one which undoubtedly agrees with "the common sense of mankind, is laid down by "Paulus in the Digest, and has been incorporated "into the French law. He says, that if a creditor "receive, by mistake, any thing in payment, dif-"ferent from what was due, and upon the supposi-"tion that it was the thing actually due: as if he "receive brass instead of gold, the debtor is not "discharged, and the creditor upon returning that "which he received, may demand that which is "due by the contract."* This has been also formally settled in Massachusetts.† Still more recently in the English court of Common Pleas,‡ it

* 2 Johnson R. 459. † 6 Mass. Reports, 183. ‡ 5 Taunton R. 488.

has been decided upon argument, that a person who discounts a forged navy-bill for another who presented it to him ignorant of the fraud, may receive back his money, and so too may he who receives forged bank-bills in payment.

I might add to these many insulated cases in the courts of common law on both sides of the Atlantic, where the gross injustice which would otherwise result, has compelled judges to rule in direct contrariety to the analogy of the ordinary law of sales and contracts, but in unison with the every-day notions of common honesty.

But quite enough has been adduced to show, that these rules have been recognised as just in the highest courts, and the most important causes; and what is of more consequence, that they have been proved to be practical, useful, and politic, by half a century's constant practice in insurance, in the equity jurisdiction over contracts, and, occasionally, in the law of sales.

It is equally certain that another, and that the older and more extensive part of our legal system, is in direct opposition to these views. Perhaps this very fact is the highest attestation that can be devised of their truth and wisdom. The power of habit and prejudice, the weight of authority, the analogy of the law, all combine to exclude them; yet, in numberless instances, (to make use of the remarkable words of one of the wisest magistrates and ablest lawyers who ever presided in the courts of Great Britain,) "necessity and convenience have required equity to break in upon the common law."*

If, then, these principles are just in themselves; if they are congruous to the common notions of men; if they are capable of being practically applied; if, in the affairs of the greatest magnitude and interest, they have been found not only expedient to be used as legal rules, but even absolutely necessary, why should they not be universal? why should that part of our law which enters into and affects every man's daily concerns, be disgraced by contradictions which, if they were nothing more than deviations from the rest of the system, would be useless and perplexing?

How much worse, if these deviations afford shelter for dishonesty, if they are repugnant to the usages of trade, and the common reasonings of civilized men?

The Roman law and the present practice of the greater part of the civilized world, give a still greater and more positive support to the value of these doctrines as legal rules. On every point touching the due execution of contracts as respects kind, quality, or intrinsic defects, in all that relates to the implied warranty of title, of soundness, and all material facts affecting the use of the thing

* Lord Hardwicke in Watley v. Berkhead 2 Vesey, 571.

sold, the principles above insisted upon, have been fully recognised, and developed according to local usages, and the custom of trade, (*ut mos regionis postulat*,* as the code expresses it,) with the greatest accuracy in all the systems founded upon the jurisprudence of Rome. In France, Holland, and many of the states of Germany, and the north, every point of their legislation is in direct opposition to the common law doctrines of sale.

For centuries, some of the most busy and commercial nations of the earth have acted upon these principles, and in this way given the most satisfactory and unanswerable proof of their fitness for the regulation of trade, and the administration of justice.

In the United States, one of our most commercial states, that of Louisiana, has long governed its active and various trade by the civil law maxim of *caveat venditor*, applied nearly in the same manner as in the present French code. With the modifications and limitations necessary to their peculiar state of society, and their principal articles of traffic, it has been found, in practice, say the lawyers and men of business of New-Orleans, to be

* The recognition of the custom of trade, or local usage, (*mos regionis* in the language of the civilians,) as a rule of interpretation of contracts, and the considering bargains as made with a silent reference to the custom, though they have obtained a footing in the common law, seem to be much more consistently acted upon in the civil

"of excellent use in repressing bad faith, and the contrivances of fraud, and in protecting the unwary against the deceitful and cunning. There is not that stimulus to fraud which arises from throwing the burthen of caution on a purchaser who does not, and cannot be supposed to know the qualities or the title of the thing which he never had in possession; nor is the sense of justice there shocked by permitting a deceitful vendor to retain the full price for an article of inferior value."*

On other articles of the law of commutative contracts, as to reservation regarding extrinsic circumstances affecting price, the Roman law and the codes of the continent, have scarcely gone so far in practice as the equity courts of our own system; but they allow our doctrines in theory, and only err in too vague and extravagant an over statement of them, to allow them to be rigorously applied. The manner in which this has been done has been already sufficiently explained.

I trust that enough has now been said to show, that these doctrines have the sanction of experience. They have been tried as legal rules, long and variously, and their utility has been found as great as their justice is clear.

* I quote from some well written and judicious letters on the law of Louisiana, as compared with that of those states following the common law, which appeared in the New-York Review for October and November, 1825, while this volume was printing. They are by Charles Watts, a lawyer, bred up in the school of common law, but now practising in New-Orleans.

Let us next cast a rapid glance on the other side of the question, and inquire what is likely to be the result, and what, in fact, it has been, where artificial system and positive regulation, have been substituted to the rules of natural equity.

CHAPTER VIII.

View of the practical result of those doctrines of Equity and Law, arbitrarily varying from the rules of natural justice. Their confusion and contradiction—their bad practical effect and evil influence on public morals.

Upon the most superficial examination of our jurisprudence, every one must be struck with the singular incongruity, that while it obstinately refuses redress in so many, and such marked instances of unfairly obtained advantages, and throws the burden of all mistakes, as well as that of the proof of positive fraud, upon the unfortunate buyer, it should yet in some of its courts, occasionally permit contracts to be set aside upon the ground of inadequacy of price, and there, require that imaginary equality between the worth of what is bought, and what is given for it, which is known only to theoretical writers, and of which the common law elsewhere denies the existence.

Suppose either of these doctrines to be sound and wise; yet the incongruity of their both being held together, is sufficient to throw uncertainty over the legal effect of the most important transactions. Let us, however, consider them singly.

What has been the result of the attempt in Equity to enforce the doctrine of equality of price being necessary to a fair bargain? Wherever the courts have lost sight of the plain distinction that insufficiency of price means nothing at all, except relatively and by comparison, and that it can have no effect upon the fairness of any bargain, unless from that comparison it affords a fair legal presumption of fraud, or oppression, or gross error as to facts, their decisions have been capricious, confused, and contradictory beyond those of any other head of equity.* But supposing that this had not been the case,—supposing that the whole system had been clear and consistent, whether right or wrong,—what would ensue? In every contract of any magnitude, not instantly carried into execution, the plain intention and meaning of a bargain honestly made, and entered into with full knowledge of all necessary facts, would, upon every fluctuation of public or private affairs which might make it inconvenient for either party to perfect his agreement, be liable to be set aside, in conformity to the opinions, the caprice, or it may be, the ignorance of a Chancellor or Equity court.

There is scarcely any subject upon which the opinions of intelligent and well informed men are

* For the detailed proof of this, I must once more refer the reader to the decisions and dicta collected by the court and counsel, in the case of Seymour *v.* Delancy. See 6 Johnson Ch. R. & 3 Cowen R.

more likely to differ, than in regard to the prospective worth of unsettled lands in this country.

One chancellor has a high opinion of the future value of our wild western land ; another who has long held unproductive property of that kind, may be very incredulous as to its speedy rise. How widely different would be the decision of these two, respecting one of those contracts for the sale of lands, so common in this country !

An English nobleman, the other day, agreed to give ten thousand guineas for a race-horse. The horse might have been sold at that price to twenty others, and was worth perhaps nearly as much in actual gain to the owner. Imagine that before the money was paid, Memnon should be beaten and lose his reputation, or that for any other reason the Peer desired to get rid of his bargain. The parties appeal to such a Chancellor, as Pothier is described to have been, learned, upright, and wise, but living in the retirement of a small town, buried in books and papers, and ignorant of all the usages of men. He would indeed, " lift up his hands and eyes in astonishment," in exact conformity with the very logical and precise rule of our law, and at once pronounce this to be a clear case of inadequacy of price, making the bargain " hard and unconscionable," and not to be sustained in equity.

Bring the same case before Thurlow, a man as familiar with the amusements and follies as with the graver business of life, and he would have treated the defence with surly contempt, and compelled the peer to pay his money and take his horse.

In this way equity would become in fact, what old Selden, in the jealous spirit of a common lawyer long ago accused it of being: "A roguish thing: "It is according to the conscience of him that is "Chancellor, and as that is larger or narrower, so "is equity. 'Tis all one as if they should make the "standard for measure a Chancellor's foot; what "an uncertain measure would that be! One Chan- "cellor hath a long foot, another a short foot. 'Tis "the same thing in the Chancellor's conscience."

The anomalies of our law regarding the concealment of external facts, have been indicated in a former chapter. How perplexing is it that an advantage is allowed to be taken in the sale of a ship or its cargo, which in an insurance of the same thing between the same parties is pronounced fraudulent! How unsettling is this contradiction to all those notions of private morality, which, it is, if not a primary, certainly an important function of the law to impress upon the people! What a door too, does this open to successful roguery! If it is the first duty of the law, *cives integros, incolumesque servare** —to protect the innocent citizen against the injuries of the artful—here clearly our law often fails to discharge its duty faithfully and completely.

* Cicero.

Next turn to that part of our common law doctrine of sales, which, on the other extreme, demands an actual warranty to charge the seller for intrinsic defects or differences in kind or quality so great as essentially to vary the bargain from that in contemplation of the parties.

There is no part of the law of the land, where it is of so much importance as it is in the law of sales, that rules should be well settled and generally known. Other principles touch the concerns of the citizen but now and then; he is subject to the regulation of this head of the law, every time that he buys, sells, or bargains. The rule, that the buyer must stand to all risks, except there has been a stipulation to the contrary, or a positive lie used, seems clear and intelligible enough. Yet whether it be because it is in opposition to the common practice of mankind, or from the numerous cases of hardship and injustice to which its rigid application gives rise, nothing is more evident than that the law has ever been vacillating, and irregular, and oftentimes obscure. Anciently the rule was rigidly enforced; then the opinion that a sound price warranted sound goods, crept silently in, and was practically the law of England for a long while. This was overruled, and the old doctrine re-established in full force about thirty years ago. Of late, again, the courts of Westminster Hall appear to relax it, by making very slight circumstances of description, as well as the custom of trade imply or amount to a warranty.* Still the point to which this relaxation reaches is very dubious. It is ruled, in one case, that a description of goods in a bill of parcels amounts to a warranty; and in another, by the same judge, that the name of a great artist printed in a sale catalogue opposite to the name and number of a picture, is merely a description which has nothing to do with the bargain. In no part of the law, certainly in none equally simple, are there more cases overruled, doubted, distinguished, or explained away in after decisions.

In the United States, the several state courts who cite the same books, and are governed by the same rules, vary yet more widely as to all practical purposes. In New-York, the rule of *Caveat Emptor*, is carried farther than can well be reconciled with the recent English decisions; or if the New-York cases can be reconciled with them, it must be by legal ingenuity, and not by any plain distinction intelligible to a plain man. In Massachusetts, the late Chief Justice Parsons frequently mitigated the severity of the law, by implying and presuming warranties where no express stipulation had been made. In South Carolina, the common law of

* Among the examples in the more recent books, see 1 Starkie, 502. 4 Campbell R. 144. 1 Moore R. 106. and 4 Taunton R. 347. In the latter case, Judge Heath says, that in an action on the sale of sheep sold as stock, the evidence being that by the custom of trade stock was understood to mean sound sheep, he directed the jury that this was an implied warranty that they were sound, and this direction, he says, was never doubted.

sales has been still more widened, yet without being quite rejected.

In addition to the modifications and irregularities thus introduced by time and place, there are every here and there, in all the courts, decisions and rules on special points which are wholly and irreconcilably at variance with the prevailing spirit of the system. The necessities of commerce and of the paper currency of modern times have, among other things, taken bank notes altogether out of the rule; as has been mentioned in the last chapter. There may be good reason for this; yet it is a legal anomaly, and from that circumstance alone, likely to mislead and to do as much harm as it does good.

Besides this; the man who buys a coat or a horse, takes it as it is, and if without the fault of the seller the coat is ill made, and the horse lame, the buyer has no remedy. But, says Blackstone,* "there "is an implied warranty with the farrier, that he "shoes a horse, not only to the best of his ability, but without laming him; with a tailor, that "he performs his business in a workman-like manner; in which if they fail, an action lies to recover damages for the breach of their general undertaking."

There is yet a more singular anomaly. It is

* 3 Blackstone Com. 165.

said by Blackstone to be law,* and it has been solemnly decided in New-York and Massachusetts, that in contracts for provisions for domestic use, it is always implied, that they are wholesome; if they are not so, an action lies to recover damages. "In a sale of provisions for domestic use," say the Supreme Court of the state of New-York, "the vendor is bound to know that they are sound and wholesome."†

I am obliged to confess my utter inability to ascertain what are the provisions and the kind of unsoundness that fall under this rule. Spoilt beef certainly does, but damaged wheat, sour flour and wine, or bad liquors, do not; at least so I infer from a hasty examination of some of the cases.

The alleged ground of the rule is the necessity of guarding the public against the sale of things injurious to health and life. No one can deny this to be a good reason, in itself; but we may judge of its consistency with the rest of the law, when we recollect that no such responsibility attaches to the seller of the ship or boat, the horse or carriage, whose unsoundness may drown you, or break your neck; nor to the seller of a steam-engine, or of a gun whose bursting may be just as fatal; nor to the vendor of the drugs which are to be taken as

* 3 Bl. Com. 166.

† 12 Johnson R. 468, and so ruled in Massachusetts.

medicines, and may prove poison; nor of liquors in general; nor, finally, to the seller of the very same beef and pork not bought in single pieces from the market, but barrelled up in quantities as an article of merchandise, when, instead of spoiling the dinner of a family or two, it may spread disease and death through whole fleets and armies, prisons and hospitals.

While there occurs such frequent collision between the jurisprudence of states speaking the same language, and courts professing to be governed substantially by the same law; that opposite doctrine which has been adopted by the civil law, is so homogeneous and intelligible, that the opinion of any Paris lawyer of good repute at the long famed Pillar of Consultations in the *Palais*, upon any question of implied warranty, with a full statement of facts, would be received as good law at New-Orleans and Dresden. The simple reason of this uniformity in one system, and these vacillations in the other, is to be seen in the fact, that the one, by the confession of all, agrees with the common understanding and usage of men, the other is the offspring of artificial and positive law.

But the wisdom and policy of the artificial rule has been asserted boldly, and defended with ingenuity, by a legal writer of high and deserved reputation, Fonblanque, in his treatise on Equity. His argument has been cited with marked approbation, and adopted as their own, by some distinguished American judges.*

Mr. Fonblanque thus argues:

"The principles upon which courts of law proceed upon the subject of warranty, so strongly "tend to reconcile the claims of convenience with "the duties of good faith, that I cannot conceive "the means by which they can receive an additional extent, or be in any degree circumscribed, "without endangering the interests which they "are now so well calculated to preserve. To excite that diligence which is necessary to guard "against imposition, and to secure that good faith "which is necessary to justify a certain degree of "confidence, is necessary to the intercourse of society. These objects are attained by those rules "of law, which require the purchaser to apply his "attention to those particulars which may be "supposed within the reach of his observation and "judgment; and the vendor to communicate those "particulars and defects which cannot be supposed "to be immediately within the reach of such attention. If the purchaser be wanting of attention "to those points where attention would have been "sufficient to protect him from surprise or imposition, the maxim caveat emptor ought to apply;

* As by Judge Thompson in 2 Caines' Rep. 54, who says: "I see no injustice or inconvenience, resulting from this doctrine; but on the contrary, think it best calculated to excite that caution and attention which all prudent men ought to observe."

"but even against this maxim he may provide, by "requiring the vendor expressly to warrant that "which the law would not imply to be warranted. "If the vendor be wanting of good faith, *fides ser-* "*vanda* is the rule of law, and can scarcely be "more effectually enforced in equity than it is at "law."*

This ingenious apologist, like many other apologists, has here a little varnished over and improved the system he defends. It is not so clear, as he states it to be, that in the common law the "vendor is obliged to communicate the defects not within the reach of the buyer's attention." But let this pass. The argument is plausible, and to a certain extent it is true. Between fair dealers, if the law is well settled and universally known, this rule may be as equitable as any other, since all contracts would be made with a secret reference to it. If it is not so known, none of the good effects which are spoken of, can be hoped for. Now, in fact, this rule is not known, nor have we any right to expect that it should be known to all classes whom it may reach. It contradicts the habits of thought and of dealing, which all of us grow up with from our childhood. Even those to whom it is known, never think of applying it, except when they feel that they are dealing with sharpers, or persons to be kept at arms' length; or

* Fonblanque, Treatise on Equity, I. 379

where, from some peculiar custom of trade, (such for instance, as exists among us in buying horses,) every man has warning to take care of himself. In our common purchases for personal use, every man takes it as much for granted that the goods he buys at retail are merchantable, as if he had an express warranty from the tradesman.

No man in buying for the daily consumption of his family ever thinks of asking for a warranty, or providing for the evidence of a representation. In effect, to do this, without some very special reason, would be to express a suspicion that the man you deal with is contriving to cheat you.

We may safely appeal to every one's observation, that this is the case. It is so even here among the intelligent and commercial inhabitants of New-York, where the common law in its strictness has been so repeatedly settled and enforced by judges enjoying the highest reputation for learning and ability.

A volume of reports published since this essay was put to press, affords me additional and conclusive evidence that this doctrine of sales never does become familiar to the people, so as to enter into their contracts, and enable them to guard against fraud.

Not long ago it was solemnly, though not unanimously, decided upon argument by the Supreme Court of Connecticut, that the sale of a chattel for a sound price did not amount to a warranty that the thing sold was merchantable in quality. Reports in that state being of recent date, this is the first reported case on that point in Connecticut. In this case, one of the judges observes that, "for "a long course of years in this state there was an "implied warranty, as to quality, supposed to be "attached to every sale where the vendor received "a sound price."*

Now in no state or district governed by the common law, is there to be found a population so well informed as that of Connecticut is, as to all their rights, legal, personal, and political; so universally and proverbially prudent as to their interests, or among whom the tenure of property, the modes of business, and the more popular and useful rules of law are more familiarly known by the mass of the community.

For the last sixty years justice had been administered among them by a succession of judges eminently enjoying and deserving the respect of their fellow citizens. Some of these have afterwards risen to the first honours of the nation. In their Superior Court had presided the clear-headed Roger Sherman, the Fabricius of our revolution, *abnormis sapiens*,—Oliver Elsworth, afterwards Chief Justice of the United States, and one worthy to succeed Jay, and to be the predecessor of Marshall—

* 4 Conn. Rep. 434, by the late Judge Chapman.

William Samuel Johnson,* a lawyer trained at the feet of Mansfield; like him, fraught with various learning, and the widest range of legal science; like him, wise and eloquent.

If with such judges, and among this acute, well informed, and busy people, the law of sales never could become known and familiar, it is in vain to attempt making it so any where else. Besides this, supposing the general rules known as well as any arbitrary rule of law can ever be; still, to all but the bar, the distinctions and contradictions which attend it must ever remain a mystery. None but a lawyer will ever comprehend that there can be one legal rule for the sale of provisions, and another for the sale of other matters: that there is an im-

* This distinguished man, to whom the political and legal institutions of this country, as well as its learning, are deeply indebted, passed a number of years in England, between 1760, and 1768, as the agent extraordinary of the colony of Connecticut, for the management of a great land cause of much interest to the province. Here he became both personally and professionally acquainted with Lord Mansfield, saw him in private life, and lost no opportunity of studying him as a lawyer, by diligent attendance at Westminster Hall, and the circuits. He continued to cherish his admiration for this great man to the last hour of his long life. From him, the guide and instructer of my youth, I early imbibed a veneration for the name of Mansfield, which all subsequent studies of my own have contributed to confirm and increase. It requires but a slight effort of the imagination to raise him up before me—not indeed, quite such as Pope knew him, the elegant and accomplished Murray,

> "Noble and young, who charms each heart
> With every sprightly, every graceful part;"

but such as he was some years later, in the meridian lustre of manly beauty, and genius, and eloquence, as Cowper tells us he remembers him, "wonderfully handsome, and expounding the most mysterious intricacies of the law, or recapitulating both matter and evidence of a cause as long as from here to Eartham, with an intelligent smile playing over his features, which showed with what perfect ease he did it."

plied warranty of bank notes and money that they are not counterfeit, but none as to gold or silver in bullion; to say nothing of the numberless other obscurities and doubts yet remaining to be cleared up.

Therefore, granting that all this could be rendered intelligible to those whose business made it important that they should know it, why impose upon society the labour of learning an artificial system, when the ends of justice could be at least as well accomplished by another system, which the ablest judicial expounders or makers of our law concede to agree better with the common sense of mankind?*

We have thus far considered the question only as regulating contracts between men of ordinary fairness and honesty. But look at the world, such as it is, mixed up of honest and dishonest men, and of the multitude who are somewhere between the two; and then pronounce which is the wisest rule in practice. Which will most effectually prevent fraud?

Under the common law, the knavish dealer has merely to evade the giving an express warranty, or a formal representation; or, if he does give them, he has only to take care to make the evidence of it uncertain, and then with ordinary address he may safely defy all attempts to bring home to him the

* As Chief Justice Kent, in 2 Johnson R. 459, and to the same effect in 2 Caines R. 55.

scienter or the fraud. Half of the horse-causes that are tried, afford examples how easily this can be done.

Reverse the rule; make the seller, who has the means of knowing the quality and condition of his wares, responsible for their being such as the bargain shows that they must have been represented or understood to be, then all opportunity of fraud is at once cut off. In general, the seller ought to know the worth of his property as well as he does his title to it. Where he does not, it is commonly in some large commercial transaction made with deliberation between intelligent men. In such cases it is fair, and it is also very easy for the seller to liberate himself from that responsibility by stating the fact as it is; that he knows nothing of the goods but from his invoice, his bill of parcels, or the description of some former owner. Where this is not done, why should not the seller bear the penalty of his negligence or his fraud, (whichever it may be,) without imposing on others the difficult and odious task of proving a deceit in the sale?

There is another point of view in which this subject may be contemplated, and which no wise legislator will willingly neglect. It is the moral effect of the doctrine upon the community at large. It is impossible that the law of the land should not have a powerful influence upon the moral judgments and habits of life of a large class of society.

There are every where many too indolent or ignorant to think for themselves, and who unhappily have no other external monitor of duty than the law. There are many who wish to be upright, and at the same time are anxious to conciliate worldly interest with moral duty. These are commonly satisfied with themselves so long as they do or neglect nothing which the law prohibits or enjoins. There are yet others the slaves of gain or of passion, but who are still alive to the reproaches of conscience, the sense of shame, or the pride of character. To these, above all men, a law low in its moral requisitions is dangerous; it serves them for a justification of their conduct to others, for an excuse and a palliation in their own eyes.

What now is the lesson which such men are taught by the common law notion of *Caveat Emptor?*

Our Law addresses the seller thus:—

"Be honest, if you choose to be so—but at all events be cautious. Take care that no fraud can be proved upon you, and then make the best of your bargain."

To the buyer it says: "Be vigilant—consider yourself as surrounded by thieves and sharpers—trust no man—look upon every one who buys or sells as a rogue."

Oh! if the honour, the integrity, the religion that have ever accompanied that noble language which we speak, had not strongly counteracted the influence of the law, how terrible would have been its effects! Nor is it easy to say at this moment, how great a part of the too lax commercial morality of our cities, is to be attributed to this single cause.

On the contrary, the law of reason and conscience, as the civil code has practically adopted it, speaks thus:—

It says to the seller: "Be honest—do unto your neighbour as you would wish him to do unto you—be vigilant for his interests as well as your own." At the same time, it bids the buyer rely with a frank and manly confidence upon the integrity of all with whom he deals, certain that whenever he is mistaken in this, the law will protect his rights; certain too, that it will do this upon the simple proof of facts, without requiring of him the disagreeable and difficult task of branding his neighbour with the guilt of fraud.

There is now a liberal spirit of legal improvement abroad. We have recently in several of our States modified the common law of partnership, by the introduction of those limited partnerships long used on the continent of Europe.* The ancient doctrine of the rights of principal and agent, as to third parties, is also undergoing discussion and alteration on both sides the Atlantic.

* The *societe en commandite* of the French law

These changes are wise, but their benefits reach but to few compared with those whose interests are affected by the general law of sales.

No more practical or beneficial innovation can be made in our civil jurisprudence, than that of introducing the civil law rules of implied warranty of quality and kind. This should not be done piecemeal, as has occasionally been heretofore attempted, or in insulated decisions which only create confusion ;—It should be done thoroughly and upon principle.

The odious maxim of *Caveat Emptor* with all its trains of absurdities and contradictions, should be for ever expelled from our courts.

In this reform there need be nothing wild or theoretical, or experimental. All the light that can be given by long experience, by venerable authority, by judicial wisdom, is at our command. We have but to borrow from the ancient civil law, from the more modern law of Germany, France, Holland, Scotland, and Louisiana, from the English equity, from our own insurance law, those principles and rules which have grown out of the practical experience of many centuries.

By merely generalizing into universal provisions what has already been decided in numerous particular cases, these may be embodied in the language of our own system, and illustrated by the reasonings of the most venerable names of the English and American bench.

I must be permitted to add, that bad and mischievous as is the principle of the rule of *Caveat Emptor*, I am not sure that I do not dislike it the more on account of the form it bears.

It is one of that tribe of anonymous Latin maxims that infest our law. None of them have any real authority, some of them have no real meaning; and there is scarce one, where the exceptions are not nearly as broad as the rule. But they are phrases "of exceeding good command," for they fill the ear and sound like sense, and to the eye look like learning; while their main use is to supply the place of either or both. At the same time, they add very much to what is the great opprobrium of our law, the dangerous facility with which a judge or a lawyer may make it what he pleases. Thus; one maxim teaches that common error makes common law; *Communis error facit jus.* Another says that ignorance of the law excuses no one; *Ignorantia legis neminem excusat.* A case occurs where the universal custom of business is one way, and some rule or decision that has slept for centuries in the yearbooks, the other. With these two convenient and pliable maxims at hand, the judge has it in his power to decide as he pleases; the partial judge for his friend; the careless or inattentive judge, according to the whim of the moment; and the ignorant judge, (for such things are) even just as it may happen.

It is related of some political hypocrite of Oliver Cromwell's time, that he was wont to preface his speeches with "Now do I call my God to witness." On such occasions an old companion of his who knew him well was accustomed to mutter, "Now do I know that this man is about to tell some lie."

In like manner, whenever in a law report I meet with one of these mouldy scraps of bad Latin, I always prepare to find some argument or decision startling to common sense.

To return to the general argument :—

From the brief and condensed manner in which the decisions, rules, and reasoning of the law have been above stated, the reader will perceive, that with the aid of a good library, it would have been very easy for me, by fuller statement of cases and following out references, to have swelled this and the preceding chapter into bulky volumes.

But enough has been said to establish the truth of the position which I have undertaken to prove; that the rules of natural equity in contracts have been found by experience, to be the best and wisest rules of civil justice; and that every needless deviation from them leads into error and confusion in the law, unsettles men's notions of right and wrong, stimulates dishonest ingenuity by the promise of impunity, makes property insecure, and frank and fair dealing hazardous.

CHAPTER IX.

Summary recapitulation of Principles and Rules.

I SHALL now summarily recapitulate the doctrines which it has been the object of the preceding chapters to explain and defend. This will be best done by stating some leading definitions and rules, comprehending the grand principles that regulate the moral justice of contracts. They are principles, which, I have the firmest conviction, can never be contradicted by any system of positive jurisprudence, without that legal system being so far forth defective, erroneous, and unwise.

I do not pretend here to offer a formal code, or systematized project of legal reform. My object is to state principles, not to propose laws. Whilst I feel the most perfect certainty as to the truth of these doctrines, I am very far from being equally satisfied with the verbal precision of my own rules. No man who has not tried the experiment, can be aware of the extreme difficulty of stating general legal or moral propositions, without more or less ambiguity, or obscurity; and without the words literally comprehending more than was intended, or else excluding some thing meant to be comprehended within the spirit and intention of the rule. In making this attempt I have not neglected the lights of experience, and have adopted, where I could, and with no more alteration than seemed absolutely necessary, the language of our own law of insurance, and of the Roman, the French, and the Prussian codes.

So far as morals are concerned, all this is nothing more than the giving method and formal expression to the reasoning which conscientious and thinking men have already in their minds in a less definite shape.

With regard to the law; it is a humble attempt to introduce order and consistency, where confusion and uncertainty now hold their chaotic reign; and that too in a branch of law where it is every man's interest that certainty and justice should govern.

A little more than a century ago, equal, perhaps greater perplexity and contradiction, existed in a collateral head of the law, which like that of sales is interesting to all men; and like that too in its present state, was neither generally understood, nor precisely ascertained. This was the law of Bailments, which regulates the responsibilities and risks of the parties in deposites, commissions, custody after sale, lending or hiring moveables for use, and possession of goods, for the purpose of transportation, or of work to be performed upon them.

At a time when the civil law was still exceedingly odious in England, Chief Justice Holt, (a name dear to Liberty,) had the courage and the wisdom to decide a great case in Bailment, on plain and rational prineiples, and to recognise in detail the whole civil law doetrine concerning it, as being "agreeable to reason and to what the law is in other countries."*

Sixty or seventy years after, Sir William Jones, in his elegant treatise on the same subject, filled up and completed the system. The authority of Holt, and the learning of Jones, have now settled the law of bailment, upon the basis of reason and truth; so that in every case of this nature, where the facts are ascertained, the decision of the courts, and that of the law of reason and conscience, is the same.

Happy would it be, should the mind of some American Holt or Jones, in the senate or on the bench, be led to effect the same kind of reform in our general law of contracts. For my own part, I have no higher aim, than to direct public attention to this important subject.

Should I sueceed in this, I may say with honest pride in the homely, but manly language of Holt; "It is of great consequence that the law should be

* Coggs *v.* Bernard, 2 Ld. Raymond, 915.

" settled in this point, but I don't know whether I " have settled or unsettled it. However that may " happen, I have stirred those points which wiser " heads in time will settle."

The doctrine of Contracts may be thus summed up.

A CONTRACT is an agreement, by which one or more persons undertake, with one or more others, to do or not to do a certain thing.

A contract is commutative, or one of *reciprocal interest*, when one of the parties undertakes to do or to give any thing which is regarded by both as the inducement, or motive, for the giving or doing some other thing by the other party.

When the inducement on either side, or both, consists of the chance of gain or loss for either, depending upon the occurrence of an uncertain event, this is a *contract of hazard*.

The terms of most contracts of reciprocal interest are regulated with reference to value in exchange, which, when estimated in money, is called *Price*.

The *Market Price* of any thing is the ordinary price at which things of the same kind, and fit for the same uses, sell or would sell at the same time and place, among those whose demand causes their value in exchange or in sale, and those by whom they are commonly supplied.

Things wholly peculiar, or which are not susceptible of a regular supply, in proportion to the demand for them, have no market price, but their price depends solely on the wishes and means of the buyer and seller.

A price agreed upon honestly, with full knowledge of all material facts, is always a fair price between the parties; however excessive or inadequate it may appear to others.

But: If in any contract or sale the price of the thing sold, or done, or to be done, be much greater or less than the market price at which things of the same kind or quality sell or would sell, such variation will afford a legal presumption of a fraud or error in the contract or sale.*

Such a presumption is not conclusive, but is open to refutation, by proving the true reason and

* This is, I think, a more accurate and definite expression than the English law furnishes of the distinction which Hardwicke and Thurlow introduced into equity. Thurlow, while he clearly saw the value of the principle, also saw and confessed the loose manner in which he and preceding Chancellors had expressed it, and the consequent danger of error or injustice.

I have borrowed the language of the above rule in part from the Prussian code, Part I. Title XI. "Of acquisition of property."

It will be seen from the context, that by a "legal presumption," I do not mean (as perhaps the Prussian code does) what the civilians call, *Presumptio Juris et de Jure*, or, a conclusive presumption; but one capable of explanation and refutation by other evidence.

inducement for such deviation from the market price, and showing that the agreement did not proceed from fraud or error.

Good faith is essential to the obligation of contracts: he who commits a fraud in making a bargain, leaves the other party at liberty to set aside the agreement, if it be not executed; or to claim to be restored, as near as may be, to the situation he was in before the bargain; provided always, that the fraud is of such a nature as to make it evident, that without it, the contract would not have been made at all, or not on such terms.

Fraud may be either *direct* fraud, or the fraud of *unfair advantage*.

Direct fraud in contracts comprehends every falsehood, art, trick, or manœuvre, practised by the one party to mislead or deceive the other concerning the subject or terms of the contract.

It partakes of the nature of fraud in contracts for either party to take an advantage of the other on any point, where it was presumed by the one party, and understood to be so presumed by the other, that no advantage would be taken; and where no such advantage could be taken, except through the means of the trust thus reposed.

This trust may be directly reposed; as in the appointment of an agent, or trustee, or guardian: and the use of such confidence by an agent or trustee, to his principal's or trustor's injury and his own benefit is fraudulent, being a breach of direct confidence.

When in any contract or sale advantage is taken by *concealment* of knowledge as to any of those *material* facts concerning the terms or the subject of the contract, which necessarily and of course enter into all calculations of price among those whose demand and supply, and estimation of value, fix the market price of similar things; this concealment is a breach of implied confidence, and therefore unfair.

These *material* facts, necessarily entering into all calculations of market price, may relate either to circumstances *extrinsic,* or to those *intrinsic* to the subject of the contract.

Extrinsic circumstances, materially affecting the terms of a contract, are those which influence the market price of such things, or their exchangeable value.

Intrinsic circumstances material to the terms of a contract, are such as relate to those *qualities* of the subject of the contract, which in similar things fit them for their ordinary use, and create the demand of those whose use or desire for such things give them their value in sales or exchange.

Circumstances *material* in their nature, are not material in degree, unless they are such, as if known, would so affect the value of the thing sold or done, in the general estimation of those whose use or estimation fixes the market price of similar things, as to make the price of the actual subject of the contract vary materially from that of other things of the same nature or use.

Concealment of such circumstances, whether intrinsic or extrinsic, if they are material in nature and degree, vitiates the contract, whenever the thing is sold, or contracted for, with reference to its ordinary uses.

When a special purpose for the thing bought or agreed for, is intended by one party, and known to be so intended by the other, it is a breach of implied confidence, to take an advantage by concealment of any such fact, as, if known, would affect the worth or value of the thing in the estimation of any reasonable man having the same object; and with regard to which, the agreement alone proves that it was presumed no advantage would be taken.

It is perfectly justifiable in bargains to use superior sagacity as to probabilities, or to apply greater skill and more accurate information, as to those facts which do not necessarily enter into the common calculations of price; and concerning which no presumption or confidence, express or implied, can reasonably be entertained, that if either party possessed superior knowledge, he would not use it.

Wherever, either by the known usage of trade, or by express words, notice is given that the sale or agreement is made at all risks, and without recourse in case of error or loss ; neither party is answerable except for positive and direct Fraud.

The responsibility of making good, injuries caused by direct Fraud, can never be disclaimed in any way.

Mutual error as to the subject of the contract, does not of course vitiate the contract : But,—

A contract or sale is not duly executed, when the thing done or delivered varies materially in kind or quality, from the kind or quality expressed or understood between the parties.

These are implied from the custom of trade and the price paid ; which if settled with reference to the market price, raises the presumption that it was understood as a condition of the contract, that the subject of it had the usual qualities, and was fit for the uses which create the market demand for such things.

The kind or quality are also implied from the avowed object of the purchaser, which, if known to the other party, raises the presumption that the subject of the contract was understood to possess the usual qualities which fit similar things for the intended use.

In all contracts of reciprocal interest, there is an implied warranty that the agreement will be duly executed; unless there be some stipulation, notice, or known usage that the contract is at all risks, except that of positive fraud.

The seller, whether of goods, of services, or of the uses of things, impliedly warrants against all secret defects of what he sells, which make the thing useless for the object for which it is avowedly intended, or for the common purposes and uses of similar things; or which so lessen those uses that the buyer would not have purchased, or only at a lower rate, if he had known such defects.

This warranty includes defects unknown to the seller, as well as those known to him.

This implied warranty does not extend to defects known to the buyer.

If defects are apparent on inspection, the law must presume that they were known to the buyer; but such presumption may be refuted by positive contrary evidence.

If the defects were unknown to the seller, and the sale in all respects honest, he may in the first instance replace the thing sold by others which will correspond with the true intent and meaning of the bargain.

If this cannot be done, he is bound either to return the price, receive back his goods or other things sold, or to pay the difference of value, and interest thereon, if any ; but no farther.

The object being to restore the parties as nearly as may be to their former situation before the bargain, if this be done, the manner is not important; but if the bargain cannot be executed according to its true intent, the wisest legal policy as a general rule, is unquestionably that of the Roman and French law, which in cases of honest error as to intrinsic defects, give the *option* of rescinding the bargain, or of recovering the difference of value to the buyer.*

If the seller knew these intrinsic secret defects, he is bound, moreover, to make good all damages resulting from the error of the injured party.

* Code Civil, art. 1644. "L'acheteur a le choix de rendre la chose, et de se faire restituer le prix, ou de garder la chose et de se faire rendre une partie du prix, telle qu'elle sera arbitrée par experts."

The Civil Law also gave the buyer the option of two remedies, one by the *Actio Redhibitoria*, the other by that of *Quanto Minoris*.

The Scotch law gives the action for annulling the contract in this case, but varies from the civil, in its policy as to the action for difference of price. See Erskine's Principles of the Law of Scotland, Book III. Tit. 3. "The insufficiency of goods sold, if it be such as would have hindered the purchaser from buying, had he known it, and if he quarrels it recently, founds him in an action for annulling the contract."

But "the action *quanto minoris*, to reduce sales on account of disproportion of price to value," is not known to the Scotch Law.

The same responsibility attaches to any party to a contract, who gains an advantage therein by fraud of any sort.

In every contract of sale the seller impliedly warrants that title or right of property which he purports to sell.

If there be no description or representation of the right or kind of property, the sale impliedly includes a warranty of full and absolute property; subject to this exception:—

When the buyer knows, from the understood custom of trade, or the law, or in any other way, that he buys not the absolute property, but the seller's right or claim.

Mutual mistake as to title, without warranty, is a ground to rescind a sale at the option of the buyer.

If the seller did not know the defects of his title, he is answerable only to make good the price paid him; if he knew them, the sale is then fraudulent; and he is answerable moreover for all damages or losses resulting therefrom.

Mutual mistake or mutual ignorance of extrinsic circumstances material to the terms of a contract, do not in strict right affect the contract, or impose any liability.

In cases of mutual ignorance or error there is no implied warranty as to such qualities of the subject of the contract, as are not ascertainable as matters of fact, but depend upon individual taste and opinion, concerning which the parties severally rely upon their own judgment.

Where, from the nature of the subject, or of the transaction, the value of the thing sold appears to have been estimated as *contingent*, (there being no fraud or concealment,) there is no implied warranty as to those facts on which the contingency depends. This is exemplified in the discounting of uncurrent bank notes, the sale of negotiable paper without endorsement, and frequently in *bona fide* sales of stock, at the current rate, though above its true monied value. Here the risk is assumed impliedly, by the buyer, while the seller is answerable only for the fraud, or unfair concealment.

Such are the general principles and rules of honest dealing in bargains, and the execution of them. To make them perfectly fit for legal direction they require more preeision and circumstantiality, and many subordinate rules under each head. Besides this, in order to be readily comprehended and easily applied, they would also need the addition of examples or of adjudged cases.

Otherwise they are the rules of strict honesty, and of wise legal policy on this head, and need no other limitations, than are common to all such principles, —those arising from the necessity of general rules of evidence, or those imposed by obvious public policy.

FINIS.

ERRATA.

Page 44, line 10, for "*subserviunt*" read "subveniunt."
183, line 10, for "have just reason," read "have no just reason."
195, line 2, for "convenience" read "conscience."
197, line 16, for "allow," read "admit."

The note on page 163, on sailor's sales, should refer to the word *Sailors*, near the bottom of page 165, to which place it should be transposed.